THE GREAT POWER CONFLICT AFTER 1945

Peter Fisher

GENERAL EDITOR Jon Nichol

Contents

Basil Blackwell

Introduction

Cartoons **A** and **B** are commenting on the world's two Great Powers, America and Russia. They both show the spreading power of America and Russia after World War II. **A** is a Western view of Russia's power. To American eyes Russia seemed bent on spreading Communism across Europe. **B** is a Russian view of the 'threat' posed by America. In the cartoon, the American Government is encircling Russia with countries friendly with America.

The cartoons are sources of evidence about the *Great Power Conflict*. What can you learn about this topic by looking carefully at **A** and **B**? They were both drawn at the time the events shown were happening. This means they are *primary* or first-hand evidence. They give ideas as to how each Great Power felt, at the time, about the actions of the other. This book is designed to help you study a wide range of primary evidence by asking questions about it, like:

What does the cartoon show?

A   This French cartoon shows the Russian leader, Stalin, spreading Communism through Eastern Europe after 1945

B   A Russian view of American policy – grasping hands stretch out from the White House towards countries like Vietnam, Korea and Turkey

What point is the cartoonist making?
What can you learn about Great Power attitudes from the cartoon?
Is the cartoon fair to both sides, or is it *biased* (one-sided)?
How useful are cartoons as evidence in learning about the Great Power Conflict?

Now look at the photograph on the front cover. Photographs are another kind of primary evidence. What can you see in the photograph? What does it tell you about relations between the Great Powers? How useful are photographs like this as evidence about the Great Power Conflict? (You can find out more about the scene in the photograph on pages 30–31 of this book.)

From the study of primary evidence you will see that America, Russia and China – the third Great Power – often had different views of the same events. Looking at the evidence can help you understand the reasons for the Great Power Conflict.

In this book you are encouraged to make decisions and judgements by 'putting yourself in the shoes' of people involved in the events described. You are also asked to think about the causes of events and the different motives for the Great Powers' actions. This means trying to interpret the events yourself, long after they have happened. You must make second-hand judgements. This process is similar to how a historian might produce *secondary* evidence, long after the events, first by a study of the primary sources and then by interpreting the events.

You will find that parts of the book are arranged for class, group or individual work. All aim to help you enjoy your work and to develop your understanding of the conflict which has divided the world for the past 40 years.

1 The Great Powers

A Recipe for a Great Power

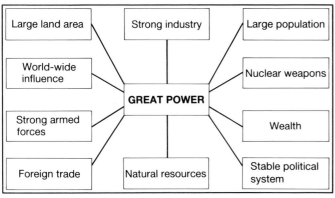

Look at the map on the inside back cover. It shows the world's Great Powers in 1984. Why are these three countries the most powerful? **A** shows what is needed to make a Great Power. America, China and Russia all have large amounts of these resources. Chart **B** gives a comparison.

Great Powers use their resources to influence other countries. They use their power to affect world events by persuading or forcing other countries to do as they wish. Often, this leads to conflict between Great Powers, even if they are not directly involved.

After World War II (1939–45) the 'league table' of Great Powers was re-drawn. America and Russia stood out as leaders of the post-war world. In the Far East, China had not yet emerged as a Great Power.

America and Russia were completely different: in history, geography, politics and economics.

B A comparison of resources

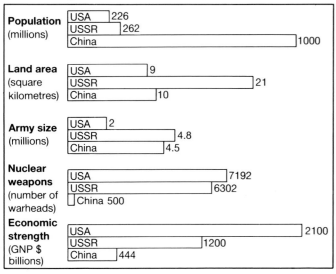

America had a short history. Its geographical position made it secure, making the American people feel strong and safe. America had strong industries, efficient farming and much overseas trade. These things made America the richest country in the world.

Russia had a long history. Though huge in size, Russia had an unsafe Western border, across which many invaders had come. Russia was rich in natural resources but its industries and farms were not yet fully modernised.

It was in politics and economics that the two countries differed most. Each had its own *ideology*, that is, its particular views on the best way to run the country. America's political system is based on *democracy*. It has a government chosen through free elections. America's economic system is called *capitalism*. All industry and land is owned by private individuals or businesses who try to make profits out of production.

Russia's ideology is based on *Communism*. In simple terms, this means that the good of the whole society should come before individual interests. So, for example, factories are owned by the state and not run for private profit. Russia's leaders decided that a strong Communist Party, with tight control, was vital to run the country: so Russia is a one-party state. In the twentieth century Russian has modernised itself into a major world power.

The third Great Power, China, is still developing. Since 1949 China's ideology has also been based on Communism. With its huge population, China has been concentrating on modernising its farming and building up its industries. With its vast resources, China has developed, in just four decades, into a major world power.

???????????????

1 List the elements in **A** in your order of importance for making a Great Power. Give reasons for the order you have chosen.

2 Compare the strengths of America and Russia under the following headings: geography; economic power; military power (see **A** and **B**).

3 Study **A** and **B**. Is it correct to regard China as a world power? What are China's strengths and weaknesses?

2 Uneasy Allies

A   Hitler and Mussolini cower from the Allied 'thunderbolt'

In Europe, from 1941 onwards, the Allies – Britain, America and Russia – were united in a common aim (see **A**). With three major powers fighting together, defeat for Hitler's forces was just a matter of time. The Allied leaders were Winston Churchill (Prime Minister of Britain); Josef Stalin (leader of the USSR); and Franklin Roosevelt (the American President). They were known as the Big Three.

The Allies needed each others' help. Britain and America depended on the Russian Red Army to wear out German forces on the Eastern Front. Russia needed American aid to keep this struggle up. The Russians relied on British and American troops invading Western Europe. This would stretch the German forces in two directions. Russian help would be needed to defeat Japan once Germany surrendered.

Beneath this surface of friendship and co-operation all was not well. Disagreements amongst the Allies developed. They differed about how to win the war in Europe, and about how to keep the peace once the war was over. As well as this, there was suspicion caused by Communist and capitalist countries working together for the first time ever.

There was deep mistrust between the Americans and Russians because of their different *ideologies* (see page 3) – although, surprisingly, Roosevelt seemed to trust Stalin. Britain also disliked Communism. Churchill did not trust Stalin, and he had made his feelings clear. Even amongst the capitalist Allies there were tensions. The Americans were suspicious of Churchill's aim to re-establish Britain's vast overseas Empire, once the war was over.

Roosevelt's main aim was to end the war. He felt that discussions about lands captured from the Germans could wait, but he did want America to play a part in the post-war world. In 1941 Roosevelt spoke of the basic rights of all men, the *Four Freedoms*: freedom from want; freedom of speech; freedom of religious belief and freedom from fear. He hoped that the future would be based on such ideas.

Stalin's main idea for the future was to protect Russia. Some 20 million Russians had died in the war. Stalin was determined that Russia should never again suffer attack from the West.

The Allies' main distrust arose over the 'Second Front' in Europe. The 'D-day' landings did not take place until June 1944. Stalin was deeply suspicious of why the invasion was delayed for so long. Perhaps, Stalin wondered, America and Britain hoped to see Nazism and Communism destroy one another?

In spite of these disagreements, the war in Europe drew to a close in 1945. The future of Germany and its conquests in Eastern Europe had to be sorted out. The Big Three met at Yalta, in Russia, in February 1945. Surprisingly, perhaps, much was agreed (see **B**).

On 7 May 1945 the German forces surrendered. The war in Europe was over, but in the Far East, Japan still fought on against the American and Commonwealth forces.

B   Results of the Yalta Conference

> The Allies agreed that:
>
> - Germany was to be divided into four zones of occupation – one each for Britain, America, France, Russia
> - Berlin was to be split up in a similar way
> - Nazism was to be destroyed and its leaders tried
> - Germany was to pay *reparations* (compensation) for war damage (half of this to go to Russia)
> - Countries in Eastern Europe were to have free elections
> - Russia was to declare war on Japan
> - A United Nations Organisation should be set up to keep peace

3 Origins of the Cold War

As the war in Europe ended, Britain and America became more and more worried about Stalin's motives. The Red Army, six million strong, remained ready for war. Russia controlled 100 million East Europeans (see map **C** on page 6). What was going on in Poland, Rumania, Hungary and Bulgaria? Was the defeat of Germany the first step in a plan to take over Europe?

Winston Churchill wrote to the Americans:

❛ *The Soviet Union has become a danger to the free world. A new front must be created against her onward sweep. This front in Europe should be as far East as possible . . . . A settlement must be reached on all major issues between the West and East in Europe before the armies of democracy melt.* ❜ **(A)**

The Big Three met for the last time at Potsdam, near Berlin, in July/August 1945. Churchill had lost power in Britain and had been replaced by Clement Attlee. Harry Truman, the new President, spoke for America. Stalin remained as secretive and determined as ever. Little was agreed. Relations between America and Russia got worse.

In the East, Russia stripped Germany of its industries. Millions of Germans were forced out of what now became Poland. Without agreement, the Russians pushed the Polish frontier westwards, deep into Germany, and set up a Communist government in Poland.

After meeting Stalin, Truman wrote:

❛ *The personal meeting with Stalin enabled me to see what the West had to face in the future. Force is the only thing the Russians understand. Stalin showed what he was after . . . the Russians were planning world conquest.* ❜ **(B)**

Was this really the case? Or were the Soviet actions simply for Russia's self-defence, as Stalin said?

The atom bomb became a vital factor. Truman had kept news of the weapon from Stalin until 11 days before its use. America had made it clear that its secrets would not be shared. This gave America a 'trump-card' and increased Russian fears. Would the West attack to destroy Communism? A deadly new era dawned. It was called the *Cold War*. C shows its main causes.

The 'Cold War' first developed in Europe – and in Germany in particular. It was a 'war' because it had two sides: America and her allies against Russia and her allies. It was 'cold' because there was no direct fighting. But all the other features of warfare existed. There were causes, armies, weapons, tactics, leaders, events and

C   Causes of the Cold War

- American fear of Communist attack
- Truman's dislike of Stalin
- Russian fear of America's atom bomb
- Russia's dislike of capitalism
- Russia's actions in the Soviet zone of Germany
- America's refusal to share nuclear secrets
- Russia's expansion west into Eastern Europe
- Russian fear of American attack
- Russia's need for a secure Western border
- Russia's aim of spreading world Communism

results. The world's two Great Powers feared each other. Each thought that the other wanted to destroy its way of life. This led to hostility, suspicion, quarrels, competition and threats. But neither side dared risk the prospect of 'hot' war.

During these years each side interpreted the other's actions in its own way. What one side saw as self-defence the other saw as aggression. This makes study of the Cold War difficult. Finding out what happened is easy enough. Working out the motives, or reasons, for the Great Powers' actions is more difficult. The very nature of the Cold War, with its climate of mistrust and suspicion, creates problems. What actually happened was often less important than what people at the time *thought* had happened!

??????????????

1 a What do you understand by the terms: Ally; Western Allies; Wartime Allies?
b In what ways, from 1941–45, did the Allies rely upon each other?

2 Why was Churchill so concerned about Russian actions in Eastern Europe (**A**)? Does the evidence support his fears?

3 Were Russia's actions in Eastern Europe self-defence or aggression? Give reasons for your answer.

4 List reasons why:
a America feared Russia in 1945;
b Russia feared America in 1945.

5 Explain in your own words what is meant by the term 'Cold War'. What were the main causes of the Cold War in 1945 (**C**)? Which of the world leaders (Churchill, Stalin, Truman) was most responsible for starting it?

4 The Iron Curtain

A Armed guards scan the iron curtain from an East German watch tower

Hans Hossfield came home from a Russian prisoner-of-war camp in 1948. He got a shock. His house, at Phillipsthal in Germany, was in a zone controlled by the Western Allies. But his family business, a printing works attached to the house, lay in the Russian zone of Germany. A frontier post lay just beyond his front doorstep. Russian sentries patrolled outside. His house lay right across the border.

Hans did not want his family to live in the Russian zone. He began to smuggle bricks into the house at night, in rucksacks. On New Year's Eve, 1951, he built a brick wall inside his house, cutting it in two. By daybreak it was finished. It took the sentries by surprise. Hans' family still live in one half of that house – as West Germans. The walled-off part, now in East Germany, is empty and decaying.

The border between East and West in Europe is called the Iron Curtain (**A**). Winston Churchill first used this phrase, in the early days of the Cold War. He was speaking at Fulton, Missouri (USA) in March 1946:

❝From Stettin in the Baltic, to Trieste, in the Adriatic, an iron curtain has descended across the continent. Behind that curtain . . . all are subject to Soviet influence and a very high measure of control from Moscow.❞ (**B**)

Was this a declaration of Cold War? Some thought so. Churchill hoped to alert the Americans to Russia's control of Eastern Europe. Russia tightened her grip in the East, between 1945 and 1947 (see **C**). Elections were held. One by one, Communist parties came to power. The West thought that these elections were 'rigged', and suspected that the leaders of rival parties

C The Soviet takeover of Eastern Europe

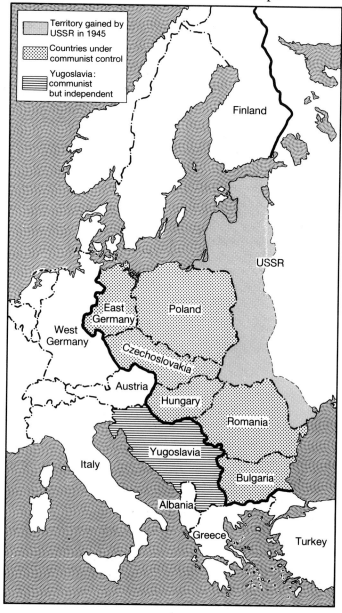

were arrested and executed. The Russians said that the people of Eastern Europe had voted with a free choice. Whatever the truth of the matter, the fact was that Russia, for the first time ever, had got a line of friendly countries across Eastern Europe. This 'buffer zone' protected her western border.

Could the West have stopped the Soviet take-over of Eastern Europe? **D** compares the numbers of land forces commanded by East and West in Europe. President Truman was under pressure to 'bring the boys back home'. The people of Britain and America would not even consider another war. After all, the Russians had just been their allies! There was nothing the West could do.

At first, the iron curtain was only a 'barrier of ideas'. It split Europe into a Communist East and a non-Communist West. It stopped co-operation and the exchange of information. It did not stop the movement of people. A tidal wave of refugees flowed westwards (**E**). To start with, in Germany the iron curtain was just like any other frontier. Many people lived and worked in different zones, with few problems.

In May 1952 Communist East Germany decided to block off its western border. Guards erected barbed wire along the border, for protection against 'spies, terrorists and smugglers'. The real reasons were different. First, East Germany was worried about the number of skilled workers fleeing to the West. Second, the East Germans were worried about the spread of non-Communist ideas into their 'workers' and peasants' state'. Soon, the only safe route between East and West was in Berlin, where the boundary stayed open.

Elsewhere along its 1400-mile length, the modern features of the iron curtain quickly developed. In a recent book, journalist David Shears describes it:

D   Land forces in Europe

1945		
West	USA	3 100 000
	UK	1 321 000
	Canada	300 000
East	Russia	6 000 000

1946		
West	USA	391 000
	UK	488 000
	Canada	None
East	Russia	6 000 000

‹ *Mines laid in double or triple rows extended along more than half of the border enclosed between twin wire fences. Ditches, tripwire, floodlights, dogs and over 2000 watchtowers, observation posts and dugouts manned by 50 000 soldiers complete the frontier.* › (**F**)

Today the iron curtain is an ugly scar cutting across Europe. It is the most obvious visible sign of the division between East and West. On both sides, border guards keep watch day and night.

‹ *Private Naumann imagined frontier duty would be more exciting . . . A grey bus is approaching the border. He registered every moment of the vehicle. A goods train rolls by. Did something move back there? Yes, there is someone walking there . . . I know her, she is going to her allotment. Nevertheless he checks back by telephone.* › (**G**)

E   Refugees from East to West, 1949–68

1949	129 000	**1959**	143 000
1950	197 000	**1960**	199 000
1951	165 000	**1961**	207 000
1952	182 000	**1962**	21 000
1953	331 000	**1963**	42 000
1954	184 000	**1964**	41 000
1955	252 000	**1965**	29 000
1956	279 000	**1966**	24 000
1957	261 000	**1967**	19 000
1958	204 000	**1968**	16 000

??????????????

1 Use **A** to describe the problems faced by someone wishing to cross from the East to the West.

2 a Using **E**, draw a graph showing refugees from East to West Germany 1949–68.
b Why was there a sharp drop in numbers after 1962?
c Suggest reasons why so many refugees fled from East to West.

3 Imagine how the following people reacted to these events:
a Hans Hossfield arriving home;
b President Truman to Churchill's speech (**B**);
c Stalin to Churchill's speech (**B**);
d Private Naumann on patrol duty (**G**).

4 Why do you think Russia created the iron curtain?

5 From the Russian viewpoint, was Stalin justified in creating a buffer zone in Eastern Europe? Give reasons for your answer.

5 Containment

The Truman Doctrine

❝I never saw such destruction. Ruined buildings, the never-ending procession of old men, women and children . . . wandering aimlessly, carrying, pushing and pulling their belongings. I was thankful that the United States had been saved the unbelievable devastation of this war. ❞ (A)

So wrote President Truman in summer 1945.

B shows the state Europe was in after World War II. Even the victors, such as Britain, were close to economic ruin. In Eastern Europe, Stalin had already imposed Communism. To American eyes, an exhausted Europe looked vulnerable to a Russian policy of expansion.

In 1947 Europe was still not free from war. In Greece a bitter civil war was raging, between the Royalists and the Communists. Britain tried to support the Royalists, but could not afford it. So Britain asked America for help. America had no obvious interest in Greece, but saw a Communist threat there. Russia was also putting pressure on Turkey. Communism was getting close to the Middle East, whose oil supplies were vital to the West.

In March 1947 President Truman spoke out:

❝I believe it must be the policy of the United States to support free peoples who are resisting attempted subjugation by armed minorities or by outside pressure. ❞ (C)

Truman got 400 million dollars from the American Congress to help Greece. His speech became known as the 'Truman Doctrine'. But what did it mean? Truman stated that

❝the peoples of a number of countries . . . have recently had totalitarian regimes (Communist governments) forced on them against their will. ❞ (D)

By this he meant the Communist governments which had been set up in Eastern Europe. Truman described the Communist way of life as

❝based on the will of a minority, forcibly imposed on the majority. (It) relies upon terror . . . a controlled press . . . fixed elections and the suppression of personal freedoms. (He called upon) nearly every nation . . . to choose between alternative ways of life. ❞ (E)

The choice was between Communism and non-Communism. Truman's speech spelled out the reality of the post-war world. It meant that America was ready to take a major part in world affairs. The USA would send money, weapons and advisors to any country, anywhere in the world, that felt threatened by Communism.

The idea of holding back the spread of Communism was known as *Containment*. It has been the backbone of American policy ever since. But in 1947 the Truman Doctrine was yet to be put to the test. Where would America's help first be sought?

Marshall Aid

❝The seeds (of Communism) are nurtured by misery and want. They spread and grow in the evil soil of poverty. ❞ (F)

Two years after the defeat of Hitler much of Europe still lay waste. Farms and factories produced less than before 1939. Even the weather was against recovery, with a severe winter in 1946–7 followed by floods and drought.

US General George Marshall visited Europe in April 1947. He found

❝People crying for help, for coal, for food and for most of the necessities of life. The patient (Europe) is sinking. ❞ (G)

Might Western Europe fall to Communism? Communist parties in Italy and France were gaining strength. In June 1947 the Americans came up with the *Marshall Plan*. It offered American aid wherever it was needed.

B   The state of Europe in 1945

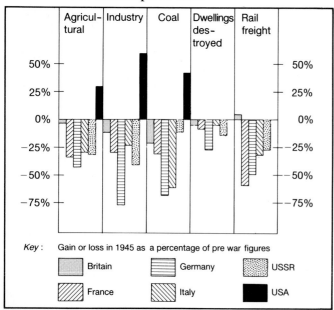

Key :   Gain or loss in 1945 as a percentage of pre war figures
- Britain
- Germany
- USSR
- France
- Italy
- USA

'Our policy is directed not against any country or doctrine but against hunger, poverty, desperation and chaos . . . Any country that is willing to assist in the task of recovery will find full co-operation (from) *the US Government . . .'* **(H)**

Was the offer of aid open to all countries, even the Soviet Union? America said 'yes' but never seriously thought that Russia would accept. **J** shows the Russian attitude to the offer. *Pravda* (the official Soviet newspaper) described it as

'a plan for political pressure with the help of dollars . . . for interference in the affairs of other countries.' **(K)**

Stalin refused to allow any Eastern European countries to share in Marshall Aid, though some, like Czechoslovakia, had been keen to take part. Western Europe jumped at the American offer (**L**). 16 countries had drawn up the Organisation for European Economic Co-operation (OEEC) to distribute American aid. Over the next four years, 13 million dollars worth of food, fertilisers, vehicles and fuel flowed into Western Europe.

Marshall Aid was the second half of Containment. By helping the recovery of Western Europe, Marshall Aid strengthened it against the threat of Communism. As Truman said,

'the Truman Doctrine and Marshall Plan were always two halves of the same walnut.' **(M)**

Marshall Aid was also good for America, since it guaranteed export markets for American factories.

Marshall Aid became a tactical weapon of the Cold War. Truman wrote:

J Part of a banner protesting against the Marshall Plan

L A West German poster welcoming Marshall Aid

'The Marshall Plan will go down in History as one of America's greatest contributions to the peace of the world . . . without it, it would have been difficult for Western Europe to remain free from Communism.' **(N)**

The Soviet view was that the plan:

'widely advertised as a 'plan to save peace', was aimed at uniting countries on an anti-Soviet basis . . . a new alliance against Communism.' **(O)**

Nowhere was the rising tension between East and West more obvious than Germany, as the following pages show.

??????????????

1 a Does the evidence in **B** support President Truman's views in **A**?

b Which country in Europe suffered most from the war (**B**)?

c Compare the fortunes of America and Russia as a result of the war.

2 Write out in your own words what President Truman meant in his speech of March 1947 (**C–E**).

3 What point is poster **J** making? Did all the Communist countries agree with this view?

4 Are **N** and **O** fair judgements of the Marshall Plan, or are they *biased* (one-sided)? How helpful would such evidence be to an historian studying the Cold War?

6 The Division of Germany

A A hungry Berliner scoops up sugar spilled by a passing lorry

Germany in 1945. A country of ruined cities and hungry, defeated, desperate people (A). In the Ruhr, police found a butcher's shop stocked with joints of human meat. Refugees were everywhere. In November, the *Guardian* reported:

❛ *Millions of Germans are on the move. Groups trek hundreds of miles and lose half their numbers through disease and exhaustion. Children have arrived in Berlin looking like the emaciated* (starved) *creatures of Belsen* (a Nazi concentration camp). ❜ **(B)**

Between 1945 and 1947, 16 million Germans arrived in Germany from Eastern Europe. One in eight (some two million) died. Much of their country was in ruins. Factories were closed, industry was shattered, farms could not grow enough to feed the people.

The Allies split defeated Germany into four zones. Berlin was divided up in the same way (see map C). Germany would be run by an Allied Control Council, made up of army leaders. It would be one economic and political unit, with joint elections held in the four zones. The Allies hoped that, in time, Germany could be reunited into a 'safe' and democratic country. Such hopes were short-lived, for soon the Allies fell out.

The first clash occurred in 1946. It was over *reparations* (compensation). Russia wanted Germany to pay for the killing of 20 million Russians and widespread destruction it had caused in the war. Stalin wanted ten million dollars from Germany. At Potsdam the Allies agreed that Russia should be given a quarter of the industrial goods made in the Western zones, in return for food and coal from the Soviet zone. Russia was also allowed to strip the factories in the Soviet zone and send their machines to Russia.

The British and Americans sent the industrial goods to the Russians, as agreed. But Russia failed to send back food and coal. So in May 1946 the British and Americans stopped sending industrial goods to the Russian zone.

More problems faced Britain and America. Should they continue to pay for food for people in the Western zones in years to come? Or should the German farms and factories be built up? The Western Allies decided to build up their zones of Germany. First, in January 1947, the British and American zones were joined together. Later, in June 1948, the French zone was added, to form one Western zone. Stalin watched these events with mistrust. Russia forced its Eastern zone of Germany to accept Communism. In the Western zone elections the Communists never gained more than 8 per cent support. The Communists failed to gain control of Berlin.

Berlin was a special case. It was 100 miles inside the Soviet zone of Germany. Britain, America and France relied on free access through the Soviet zone for road, rail and canal links with the city. Berlin was an excellent point for Russia to put pressure on the Western Allies. In 1948 Russia began to make Western access to Berlin more and more difficult. Then in June 1948 Russia cut off Berlin from Western Germany. The *Berlin Blockade* had begun.

C How Germany was divided

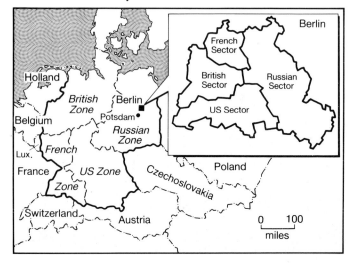

7 Berlin: Blockade and Airlift

23 June 1948. The message from the Soviet News Agency to Berlin's main newspaper ran:

❛The Soviet administration is compelled to halt all traffic to and from Berlin tomorrow at 0600 hours because of technical difficulties.❜ (A)

Berlin was cut off from the West. 'Technical difficulties' meant the Russians closed all roads, canals and railways between Berlin and Western Germany. Berlin had only enough food and fuel to last six weeks. The Russian aim was to force the West to withdraw from Western Berlin by reducing its population to starvation. The American Commander in Berlin, General Clay, said:

❛When Berlin falls, Western Germany will be next. If we withdraw our position in Berlin, Europe is threatened . . . Communism will run rampant.❜ (B)

Britain and America decided to airlift supplies into Berlin, along three narrow air corridors through the Soviet zone. The first flight, on 26 June, brought in 80 tons of milk, flour and medicine. By September, aircraft were landing in Berlin every three minutes – day and night (C).

The Berliners became desperate. By October they were allowed only small amounts of fat, spam (tinned meat), potatoes, cereal and bread. Berlin's 2.1 million people needed 4000 tons of supplies a day to survive. By spring 1949, 8000 tons were being flown in each day. In all, 2 million tons of supplies were flown in.

Why did the Russians not try to stop the airlift by military means? General Clay gave the American view

C West Berliners cheer an Allied airlift 'plane

❛The chances of war are 1 in 10. The Russians know they would be licked. If they cut our air route, they know it is an act of war.❜ (D)

To stop the airlift Russia would have had to shoot down Western planes. But Stalin was frightened of America's nuclear weapons. On 12 May 1949 the blockade was lifted.

The blockade made two Berlins: West and East. It was the end of the wartime alliance. Britain, America and Russia split into two groups, based on a West-East division. President Truman said:

❛When we refused to be forced out of Berlin, we demonstrated to Europe that we would act when freedom was threatened. This action was a Russian plan to probe the soft spots in the Western Allies' positions.❜ (E)

The Russian version was different:

❛The crisis was planned in Washington, behind a smoke-screen of anti-Soviet propaganda. In 1948 there was the danger of war. The conduct of the Western powers risked bloody incidents. The self-blockade of the Western powers hit the West Berlin population with harshness. The people were freezing and starving. In the spring of 1949 the USA was forced to yield . . . their war plans had come to nothing, because of the conduct of the Soviet Union.❜ (F)

So ended the first struggle of wills between East and West. The tactics were designed not to kill, but to threaten. This set the pattern for future Cold War conflicts.

??????????????

1 a How did the Allies divide Germany (C)?
  b What did they hope this would achieve?
  c Over what issues did the Allies disagree in 1946?

2 a What was Russia's aim in imposing the blockade?
  b Why did the Russians fail to stop the airlift of supplies to Berlin?

3 How is the Russian view of the blockade (F) different from the American view (E)? How far can we trust such evidence? Explain in your own words why the Berlin blockade was lifted.

8 NATO and the Warsaw Pact

NATO

The North Atlantic Treaty Organisation (NATO) came into being in 1949, as a result of the crisis over Berlin. America was convinced that a new military alliance was needed. In 1948 five West European countries had signed the Brussels Treaty. This included an agreement to give each other military aid in the event of armed aggression. Now a wider-reaching and stronger organisation was needed.

Russia's leaders made no secret of their views:

❝29 January, Moscow. Soviet Foreign Ministry. *The ruling circles of the USA and Britain have in the past two months been engaged in setting up a North Atlantic Alliance. It is easy to see that these aims are closely interwoven for the establishment of Anglo–American world supremacy, under the leadership of the USA.❞* **(A)**

On 4 April 1949 the North Atlantic Treaty was signed in Washington, USA. NATO had an original membership of 12: Britain, France, Belgium, Holland, Luxembourg, Portugal, Denmark, Ireland, Italy, Norway, Canada and the USA. Later members were Greece and Turkey, which joined in 1952, and West Germany, which joined in 1955 (see **B**).

All members agreed to regard an attack on any one of them as an attack on them all. All agreed to place their defence forces under a joint NATO command, which would co-ordinate the defence of the West. America was NATO's strongest member by far. America was so concerned about the threat posed by the Soviet Union that, for the first time ever, it agreed in advance to go to war on another country's behalf.

Were America's fears justified? **C** was the Russian response to the Treaty. In a note of protest, the Russian Government wrote:

❝*the North Atlantic Treaty has nothing in common with the aims of self-defence of the states, who are threatened by no-one and whom no-one intends to attack. On the contrary, the Treaty has an aggressive characteristic and is aimed against the USSR.❞* **(C)**

The peoples of Western Europe were only too glad to take refuge in an alliance backed up with the vast military strength of the USA. Ernest Bevin, Britain's Foreign Minister, spoke for millions:

❝*Like others, my country has had forced upon it the task of fighting two world wars against aggression within a quarter of a century. Today will bring a feeling of relief. At last democracy is no longer a series of isolated units.❞* **(D)**

In August 1949 the German Federal Republic (West Germany) came into being. Its territory was based on the three occupation zones controlled by the Western Allies. Bonn became its capital city. Dr Konrad Adenauer became its first Chancellor (Prime Minister).

B   NATO members and Warsaw Pact countries

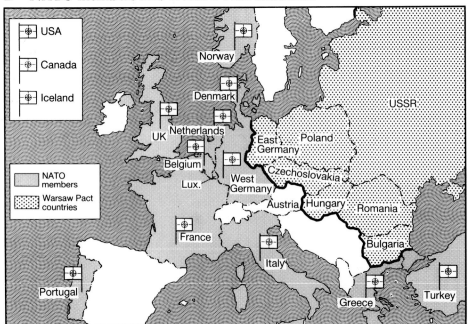

E US military bases in Britain in 1984

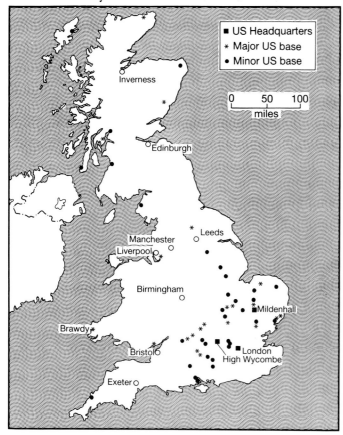

In September 1949 the Soviet zone of Germany became the German Democratic Republic (East Germany). Its capital was to be East Berlin.

Late in August 1949, much sooner than the West expected, the Soviet Union exploded its first atom bomb. East–West relations entered a deadly new phase. Today, over three decades after NATO was set up, there are still 350 000 American troops in Western Europe. **E** shows American NATO bases in Britain.

The Warsaw Pact
The failure of the Berlin blockade had far-reaching effects on Russia and the Communist countries of Eastern Europe. It was now clear that Germany could not be united. The process of creating two separate German states was speeded up.

What of the aim of German unification, agreed at Potsdam only four years earlier? Each side accused the other. The West claimed that only Russia's refusal to permit free elections prevented complete German unification. The East claimed that the West had broken the Potsdam agreement by separating-off their three zones.

Cartoon **F** shows Russia's long-standing fear. The Russians viewed the creation of West Germany as another step towards rebuilding a strong, aggressive, anti-Russian state. In 1955 Russia's worries increased

F The Russians feared that Nazi aggression would 'hatch out' again from the re-built West Germany

when the new West Germany was allowed to join NATO:

❝14 May 1955. *In accordance with the pact of friendship, co-operation and mutual assistance between the People's Republic of Albania, the Hungarian People's Republic, the USSR and the Czechoslovak Republic, the states have decided to set up a unified command of armed forces . . .*❞ **(G)**

This Treaty became known as the Warsaw Pact. It was a military treaty in which the Communist countries of Eastern Europe (see map **B**) all agreed to help each other – and the Soviet Union – in the event of armed attack from the West. In the Far East, Communist China signed as an associate member.

???????????????

1 a Why was NATO set up?
b Why did America want to join the new alliance?
c What was Russia's reaction to NATO (**A** and **C**)?
d Why did the people of Western Europe welcome the Treaty (**D**)?

2 Why do you think America still has such a large military presence in Britain (**E**) and Western Europe?

3 What reasons did East and West give for the failure to unify Germany?

4 Why were the Russians worried about West Germany joining NATO? How did the Communist countries react (**G**)?

9 China 1949—50

China. A vast nation – both in area and population. Once, China had been an important power in the Far East. But by 1900 it had become weak, backward and inward-looking. Between 1900 and 1950 the Chinese people faced serious problems (see **A**).

Despite these problems a country of China's size, population and potential could not be ignored. America and Russia both played a part in the struggle for power in China between the non-Communist Nationalists and the Communists. In this way, the focus of America's and Russia's Cold War spread from Europe to the Far East.

Throughout the 1930s and '40s, the USA backed Chiang Kaishek, the Nationalist leader. His forces were kept in power with American money, arms and advisors. The Americans believed it was vital to stop Mao Zedong's Communists gaining power.

At first, Mao Zedong looked to Moscow for help. Stalin thought that China's Communist Revolution should be like the Russian one of 1917. It should be based on the support of factory workers in towns. But

B   Mao Zedong proclaims the founding of the People's Republic of China

A   China's problems

Trade	European powers such as Britain exploited the country's trade.
Industry	Few industrial areas. Little mechanisation.
Food supply	Frequent famines caused by drought or floods.
People	A massive peasant population – very few able to read or write.
Farming	Backward. Little progress in farming methods. Mostly 'subsistence level' (peasants produced just enough to survive).
Government	Nationalist government in power, led by Chiang Kaishek. A corrupt and inefficient government. Few reforms.
Foreign invasion	1931: Japan invaded Manchuria, in Northern China. 1937: Japan invaded again. 1941–45 China fought with the Allies against Japan in World War II.
Revolution	1911: against the Emperor. China became a Republic. 1921–49: Communists, led by Mao Zedong, planned take-over from the Nationalists.
Civil War	1920s–30s: bitter fighting between Nationalists and Communists. 1946–49: Fighting began again after World War II.

China was not like Russia. Mao decided to gather his support from the millions of peasants in the countryside.

In the 1920s and '30s the Nationalists and Communists fought a bitter civil war. Between 1937 and 1945 the two sides joined together to fight the Japanese. After World War II America tried to keep the two sides together, with Chiang Kaishek in charge. But this attempt failed and civil war broke out again.

On 1 October 1949 Mao Zedong (**B**) announced

❛*We proclaim the establishing of the PRC (People's Republic of China). Our nation will enter the family of peace-loving nations of the world. It will promote world peace and freedom. Our nation will never again be an insulted nation. We have stood up. Our revolution has gained the sympathy of the masses through the entire world.* ❜ (**C**)

The Communist victory surprised the whole world. Even Russia had thought that Mao's Communists had little chance of winning the war.

Chiang Kaishek was forced to flee to the small island of Formosa (now called Taiwan). He was bitter at his defeat, and very critical of American support for his Government during the Civil War. On 9 October he wrote

World War Three has already started with Russia's direct participation in an aggressive war against China. (D)

He described the Communist Government as 'a puppet directed by Moscow' and Mao Zedong as 'the Number One traitor in Chinese history'.

The Communist success came at the height of the Cold War. To America it seemed that Mao's victory was masterminded by Moscow, as part of the Communist struggle for world conquest. Might other poor countries follow China's example and set up Communist governments – in South East Asia; the Middle East; South America; Africa? America was certain that 'containment' must now become a world-wide idea.

Russia welcomed Mao's success as a victory for 'World Communism' (E). Mao went to Moscow for talks with Stalin. In February 1950 the two countries signed a Treaty of Friendship, which was meant to last for 30 years. Russia agreed to supply China with loans, military aid and technical help to develop China's industry.

At the United Nations, Russia backed Communist China's claim to take over the 'China' seat still held by the Nationalists, but America would not agree. In protest, Russia walked out of the UN.

To America, the 'loss' of China was a disaster. America refused to recognise the Communists as the legal government of China. When Mao threatened to invade Formosa, the American Seventh Fleet protected Chiang Kaishek's exiled forces. At the UN America supported Chiang Kaishek's right to keep the China seat. In 1950 America banned all trade and travel links with China. For the next 20 years America tried to freeze Communist China out of world affairs.

America and Russia failed to realise the potential power of China and the influence of Mao. Stalin saw Mao as a junior partner. America saw Mao as a Stalin's puppet. Both were wrong.

The Chinese Revolution gave hope to millions of poor people in Third World countries. Mao, not Stalin, was to lead this new breed of Communism. As friends or enemies, Russia and America would have to take notice of the new Red Star in the East.

In 1948 Nationalist China's representative at the UN prophesied:

The fate of the entire Far East is linked to that of China. Because the Chinese Communists will help Communism in all the Far East. Against this tide, you have built up in the West a solid dyke. But now, this tide will overflow in another direction. (F)

An Eastern version of Europe's iron curtain was being created: a 'bamboo curtain'.

E The caption on this Russian poster says 'Glory to the great Chinese people who have gained freedom, independence and happiness'

СЛАВА ВЕЛИКОМУ КИТАЙСКОМУ НАРОДУ. ЗАВОЕВАВШЕМУ СВОБОДУ. НЕЗАВИСИМОСТЬ И СЧАСТЬЕ!

??????????????

1 a Why did America support Chiang Kaishek before 1949?
b How accurate was the American view that Mao's success was planned in Moscow?

2 a What does **E** suggest about the relationship between Russia and China?
b Why might Russia want to depict the relationship like this?

3 In what way was Communist China a victim of the Cold War, at the United Nations?

4 It is February 1950. Following Mao Zedong's visit to Stalin, China and Russia have signed a 30-year Treaty of Friendship. Write a brief report for an American newspaper commenting on this event, and the fact that it comes so soon after the Communists have gained power in China.

10 The Korean War 1

A 25 June – 14 September 1950

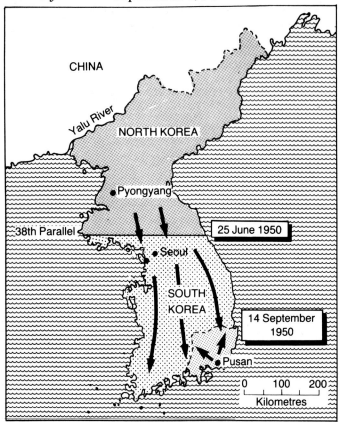

CHINA

Yalu River

NORTH KOREA

• Pyongyang

38th Parallel

25 June 1950

• Seoul

SOUTH KOREA

14 September 1950

• Pusan

0   100   200
Kilometres

Since 1910 Korea (see map inside back cover) had belonged to Japan. When World War II ended in 1945, the Allies agreed that Korea should become an independent country. Japan surrendered to Russian forces in the north of Korea, and to American forces in the south. A temporary dividing-line was drawn up along the 38th parallel of latitude (38° North). Later, it was intended that Korea should hold free elections and be re-united.

As the Cold War developed in Europe, the division between North and South Korea became deeper. Although Russia and America had withdrawn their forces, they continued to provide support – Russia to the North, America to the South. All attempts to unite the country failed. In 1948 two separate countries were set up. North Korea had a Communist government, led by Kim Il Sung. In South Korea a non-Communist state was formed, under Syngman Rhee.

The Chinese Revolution in October 1949 meant that now North Korea had two friendly Communist giants on its northern border. Meanwhile, armed forces from the North and the South began to attack each other across the 38th parallel.

On 25 June 1950 North Korean forces armed with Russian weapons invaded South Korea. In just three days they had captured Seoul, the capital of South Korea (see map **A**). Soon, Communist forces had overrun most of the country. Chart **B** suggests why the war began.

To prevent the fall of South Korea, America had to act. President Truman saw the North Korean invasion as part of a Communist plot:

‘*the attack upon Korea makes it plain beyond all doubt that Communism has passed beyond the use of subversion to conquer independent nations and will now use armed invasion and war.* ’ **(C)**

Truman moved quickly. He sent the US Seventh Fleet to strengthen Formosa (Taiwan) against possible Chinese attack. He ordered the war hero, General MacArthur, to go to Korea with military supplies.

An American motion was passed at the United Nations demanding that the North Koreans should withdraw from South Korea. Then on 27 June America put forward a second motion to the United Nations Security Council. The UN agreed:

‘*to furnish such assistance to the Republic of Korea as may be necessary to repel the armed attack and to restore peace and security in the area.* ’ **(D)**

B Why did the war in Korea begin?

Was it:	Reason
A show of Russian strength towards the Americans – part of the Cold War?	To get their own back after the 'climb down' over Berlin.
A show of Russian strength towards the Chinese?	Stalin showing Mao that *he* was the leader of Communism in Asia?
A North Korean attack planned in Moscow and backed by Peking?	It would strengthen Russia's defences in the Pacific. (America thought this was the reason.)
An independent attack by North Korea, without Russian or Chinese backing?	Because America had not included Korea in her defence plans for the Pacific?
An attack provoked by South Korea?	To regain American help against Communism. (North Korea claimed that South Korean troops had attacked first.)

16

America was only able to gain this UN backing by chance. When the Korean War began, Russia was *boycotting* (deliberately absent from) the UN Security Council. This was in protest at America's treatment of Communist China. When the UN Security Council agreed to America's demands, there were no Russians present to *veto* (stop) the decision.

The UN called upon its members to provide military forces. America's new NATO allies felt they must support America in the Far East, in return for US support in Europe. By this time, America was already involved in the Korean War. US troops formed the bulk of the UN forces, and General MacArthur was Commander-in-Chief of the whole operation.

As UN forces built up in South Korea, the Communists pressed on to capture Pusan (see map **E**). On 15 September, MacArthur's forces landed at Inchon (**F**), to attack North Korean supply routes from the rear. Bitter fighting followed. Eventually the UN forces captured Seoul. By October 1950 the North Koreans had been forced back behind the 38th parallel. Communism had been contained – so was the UN's task over?

The Americans did not think so. MacArthur and Truman saw this as the chance to unite Korea. Not content with containment, they wanted to free North Korea from Communist control.

China saw the American plans as a real threat. If UN forces captured North Korea, they might press on to attack the border with China. And they could use North Korea as a base for bombing raids on Chinese industry. The Chinese issued a warning:

❛*if the Americans cross the 38th parallel, China will be*

E 15 September – 1 October 1950

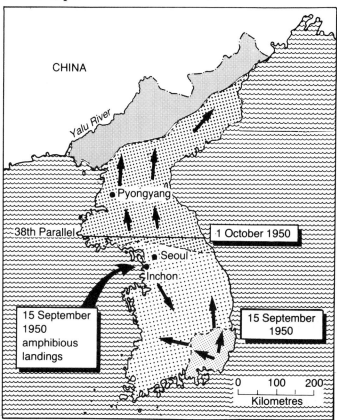

forced to intervene in Korea. ❜ (**G**)

Despite this warning, Truman ordered MacArthur to cross into North Korea on 7 October. He asked for UN support for this action, and got it. The UN forces advanced and captured the North Korean capital. Then they continued north, towards the Chinese border. Would China carry out its threat?

F American assault craft at Inchon

11 The Korean War 2

A November 1950 – January 1951

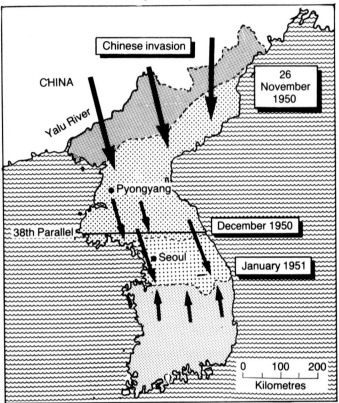

D July 1951 – July 1953

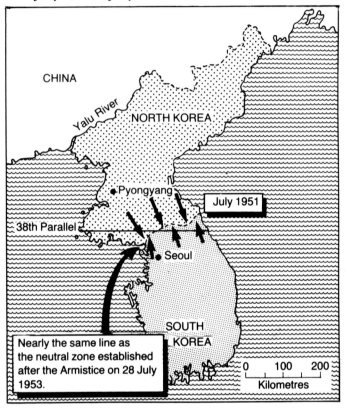

October 1950. 300 000 Chinese troops crossed the Yalu River (the border between China and North Korea, see map **A**). They were to fight alongside the North Koreans as 'Chinese People's Volunteers'. They were called 'volunteers' so that China would not have to declare war on the UN forces. Officially, the Korean War was still a Civil War between the South (with UN backing) and the North. In reality, it had become a Great Power Conflict between America (and its allies) and the Chinese Communists, who were supported by Russian weapons and advisors.

The massed Chinese armies met the UN forces and pushed them back through sheer weight of numbers. In two weeks the UN forces lost all of North Korea. By January 1951 they had been forced to retreat beyond the 38th parallel.

In February, after bitter fighting, MacArthur managed to push the Chinese back to the 38th parallel again. Losses on both sides were heavy.

President Truman was keen to set up a ceasefire along the 38th parallel, but MacArthur pressed on into North Korea. He wanted to extend the war into China itself and to defeat Mao Zedong, with the aid of Chiang Kaishek's forces. He even suggested using nuclear weapons against the Chinese.

But Truman was determined that the Korean War should not develop into a full-scale Asian War. On 11 April the London *Evening Standard* reported

❮*President Truman has dismissed 71-year-old General Douglas MacArthur from all his posts.* ❯ **(B)**

Many Americans still felt that MacArthur was right. But the American Secretary of State felt that the risks were too great:

E A leaflet dropped by Americans to Chinese troops in North Korea. The Chinese soldier, issued with poor quality Russian weapons, is persuaded to surrender

'Against the advantages of spreading the war to the mainland of China, there must be a risk of Russian intervention and of World War III.' (C)

Truman, though unpopular, stuck with his policy of containment. The war had reached 'stalemate' (D). The two sides had dug themselves into a maze of trenches and fortifications on opposite sides of the 38th parallel. In the air, there were 'dog fights' between American and Chinese pilots (the Chinese in Russian jets). American bombers pounded military targets in North Korea.

At the suggestion of the Russians, peace talks began at Panmanjom in June 1951. All hopes of winning the war, or of uniting Korea, had now vanished. The talks were complex, and often broke down. Meanwhile the war dragged on, with each side using words (E) as well as weapons. F comes from a speech made by the American Secretary of State:

'It has been charged that the forces in Korea are engaged in a pointless struggle. Nothing could be further from the fact. Their gallant, determined and successful fight has checked the Communist advance. They have administered terrible defeats to the Communist forces.' (F)

In November 1952 General Dwight Eisenhower replaced Truman as America's President. Eisenhower wanted to end the war. He tried to pressurize the Chinese into a truce, but the fighting went on. In 1953 Stalin died. Now, China could not be sure that Russia would continue to provide help and supplies. So China agreed to peace talks. An armistice was signed on 17 July 1953, but no peace treaty could be agreed. Over 30 years later, the peace talks are still going on!

The Korean War was the first war between East and West, and the second crisis of the Cold War. This time, all the Great Powers wanted to limit the war to Korea. Although none of them won, the only real loser was Korea itself (G). At the end of the war, East and West were even more hostile towards each other. The West now knew that China would act if threatened. Korea had forced America into a new role in Asia – defender of democracy against the spread of Communism. Since America had no wish to fight another Asian War, she badly needed allies.

G   The Korean War: a balance sheet

	Gains	Losses
Korea	None	Casualties (dead and wounded): 1.3 million South Korean (military) 520 000 North Korean (military) Over 3 million civilians Much industry destroyed Agriculture ruined Millions of refugees
UN	Gained respect by taking prompt, direct action Used combined force to stop aggression Achieved joint action by members	17 000 casualties Conduct of war almost entirely controlled by US Decisions weakened by power of veto
USA	Saved South Korea from Communism Containment policy seen to work against Asian Communism	42 000 casualties Defence spending went up from 12 to 60 billion dollars Failed to liberate North Korea
Russia	Achieved closer friendship with China Conflict between China and America was to Russia's advantage	Forced into expensive arms race with America
China	Gained the respect of Asian Communists Saved North Korea from America Kept a crucial buffer state on the eastern frontier Achieved closer friendship with Russia	900 000 casualties Cost of the war Failed to win South Korea for Communism Increased American protection for Chiang Kaishek in Formosa Isolated by America in trade and politics

???????????????

1 Why did war break out in Korea in 1950? Write a paragraph outlining the main causes of the war (use **B** on page 16 to help you).

2 Write notes on each of the following: **a** why America became involved in the Korean war; **b** why Russia failed to stop UN forces going to Korea; **c** why the UN (really, America) tried to 'liberate' North Korea; **d** why China sent 'volunteer' armies to Korea; **e** General MacArthur's idea of a war against China; **f** President Truman's wish to contain Communism; **g** why China agreed to an armistice.

3 a How effective is **E** as a piece of propaganda? Do you think it would persuade Chinese troops to surrender?
b Look at **F**. Do you think the US Secretary of State meant what he said? For what other reasons might he have made this speech?

4 Which of the three Great Powers gained, or lost, most from being involved in the Korean War (see **G**)?

12 The Nuclear Arms Race

A A British view of the arms race, in 1960. America and Russia fight for the lead, pursued by Britain and France

D A display of Russian missiles in the annual May Day parade in Moscow

The atom bombs dropped on Hiroshima and Nagasaki ended one war but helped start another. Nuclear arms became a vital factor in relations between the Great Powers from 1945 onwards. The leaders of the Great Powers came to realise that if the Cold War turned into 'hot war', the use of nuclear weapons would result in tens of millions of dead on either side, and the extinction of society. Yet both East and West set out on a race to equip themselves with even more lethal nuclear weapons (**A**). Why?

The awful power of the atom bomb only became clear to Americans after the first test firing, at Alamogordo, New Mexico, on 16 July 1945. One eye-witness, five miles away, wrote:

❛*The whole country was lighted by a searing light many times that of the midday sun. Thirty seconds after the explosion came first the air blast, to be followed by the strong awesome roar which warned of doomsday.*❜ (**B**)

Doomsday came to Hiroshima at 7.16 am on 6 August 1945. Out of a population of 255 000, 45 000 people died on that day, and over the next four months the total rose to 64 000. A further 72 000 people were injured. Yet within a few years bombs existed that were 2500 times more powerful than the Hiroshima atom bomb!

C gives an American view of the 'arms race' between the USA and the USSR.

1945   America has the advantage over Russia. We are the only country with the nuclear secrets for making the bomb.

Stalin is frightened of the destructive power of the bomb. No doubt Russian scientists will develop an atom bomb, but it might take them 20 years. In the meantime, America holds the trump card against any Russian threat of hot war. Our policy of containment means that we can station American bombers in countries in Western Europe. Our long-range bombers can fly 6000 miles to strike at Russia, if they have to.

1949 *September*   The Russians have exploded an atomic bomb! We did not think they could become a nuclear power so soon. We must build up our stocks of nuclear weapons against this new threat. Our scientists tell us that a superbomb' is possible – a hydrogen bomb with 2500 times more explosive power than our first atom bombs.

1950   One of our nuclear scientists has been spying for the Russians!

1952   Our first H-bomb (hydrogen bomb) test in the Pacific goes well. One H-bomb could destroy Moscow. We must concentrate on ringing the Soviet Union with bases in friendly countries. We must build more H-bombs and more bombers.

1953   The Russians have exploded an H-bomb in Siberia. They are catching up with us in nuclear knowledge! And they have a new long-range bomber. American cities could be attacked. We still have more nuclear bombs than Russia, but we must make many more and test new ones. We must deter the Soviet Union by fear of what we would do to their cities if they attacked us.

Bombers are slow – they could be shot down on the way to the target. The new H-bombs are smaller. Perhaps fighter aircraft could carry them? Or cannons . . . submarines . . . rockets?

The Russians are testing even bigger H-bombs.

1957 *4 October*   The Russians have shot a satellite, *Sputnik I*, into space – before America. The Russians are ahead in rocket development. The rocket that launched Sputnik I could be fitted with a nuclear warhead. The missiles could be fired from thousands of miles away. The Russians are building thousands of these ICBMs (Inter-Continental Ballistic Missiles). 20 million Americans would be wiped out in one day if Russia attacked. 22 million would die later, from radiation. What are we to do? Our early warning system across the North Pole is no use any more.

The Russians have many more missiles than America. Every year they show them off in Moscow (**D**). But would they use them? Our bombs can still destroy Russian cities. We must build up our missiles and bombs. Our Atlas ICBM has a range of 5000 miles at 16 000 mph. Perhaps we should concentrate on short-range nuclear weapons? They could be used across the frontiers of Europe. If it comes to nuclear war with Russia, better to destroy Europe in a limited war than America. Perhaps the Russians will agree?

1958–61   The Russians might have enough ICBMs to knock out America with one blow! We still need to be able to deter the Russians by developing 'second strike' power – to attack the Russians harder than they might attack us. We must protect our nuclear weapons from being hit by Russia's first strike. We need to develop warheads that can be fired from underground missile sites, or from mobile missile launchers.

1960 *July*   Our submarine USS George Washington has fired a new missile – *Polaris* (**E**) – from under the sea. Polaris missiles have a range of 1500 miles. Now nowhere in the Soviet Union is safe from attack from undersea submarines. The Russians are bound to strengthen their missile sites, and are developing missile-firing submarines. America may be in the lead in the nuclear arms race now, but we must stockpile more weapons in order to deter Russian attack. We need more Polaris missiles and more ICBMs. We must make use of outer space for spy satellites. We must develop defensive anti-ballistic missiles which could destroy Russia's ICBMs before they reach their target.

E   The US *Polaris* missile, during launching trials

??????????????

1 a Look at **A**. What point is the cartoonist trying to make about nuclear arms?

b What is happening to Britain and France in the race?

c Do the positions of the Great Powers' leaders give a fair view of the state of the arms race in 1960?

2 Make up a time chart like **C**, with notes explaining the *Russian* view of the arms race. Mention: Hiroshima and Nagasaki (1945); American bases in NATO countries (after 1949); the American H-bomb (1952); the Russian H-bomb (1953); the threat to Russian cities; Sputnik I; Britain's first H-bomb (1957); 'limited war'; Polaris submarines; American underground missile silos; America's stockpile of nuclear warheads.

13 Two Armed Camps 1949–55

'The matter is very simple . . . any Soviet citizen can explain it to you. The United States is surrounding us with bases which are ready to fire atomic bombs.' (A)

A was written by a Russian student in 1958. Were the Russians right to see the American bases as a threat? How had this situation arisen? *Viewpoints* should help you remember:

VIEWPOINTS

For each of the statements below ask yourself:

- Is it the view of the USA or USSR?
- What event is being described?
- What is the correct order of the events? (Clue they all happened from 1946–53)

---

1 a Churchill is stirring up hatred against us.
 b Churchill is right. What is going on in Eastern Europe?

2 a We must be strong to defend the West against Communism.
 b NATO is proof of an American threat against us.

3 a We must try to stop Communism gaining control in China.
 b They are out to destroy Communism – look at their support for Chiang Kaishek in China.

4 a At last we have a friend in China. But China is backward.
 b Mao's victory in China is a big blow. We must protect non-Communist countries in the Far East.

5 a They are out to expand into Western Europe. We must prevent this.
 b They have the bomb. We must have friendly countries in Eastern Europe.

6 a They are buying Western Europe's friendship with dollars.
 b Western Europe must be strong enough to stand up to the threat from the East.

7 a We must hold Berlin at all costs.
 b They are uniting the Germans against us. We must make our zone of Germany safe – including Berlin.

8 a They have no right to attack North Korea.
 b They are giving aid to North Korea. We must act.

Now draw up a table like this and fill in your ideas:

USA View	USSR View	Event	Year
1 b	1 a	'Iron Curtain' speech	1946

1953: What should America do?

Think about the events in **Viewpoints** through American eyes. Which of these plans would you advise President Eisenhower to follow:

1 Try to arrange a top-level meeting with Stalin, to talk about ending the Cold War?
2 Try to make treaties to surround the USSR with countries friendly to America?
3 Try to liberate the countries of Eastern Europe already under Russian control?
4 Increase America's military power by developing new weapons?

America's leaders decided on plans **2** and **4**. Between 1949 and 1955 a series of Treaties were signed between America and friendly non-Communist countries. Many of America's allies became sites for American missile and bomber bases.

1955: What should Russia do?

How would the Communist Great Powers view America's actions? Think about the situation through Russian eyes. What would you advise Russia's new leaders to do?

1 Increase spending on arms and develop new weapons to counter the American threat?
2 Make moves to lower tension by talking to America's leaders?
3 Look for friendship with Mao Zedong, in the hope of Russia and China becoming Communist allies?
4 Bind the Communist countries of Eastern Europe to the USSR in a military agreement.

Russia decided on plans **2**, **3** and **4**.

So, the decade which began with the defeat of Hitler's Germany, ended with the world re-grouped into two armed camps. It became known as a *bipolar* world – with countries friendly to America in the West and Russia in the East (B).

B A bipolar world

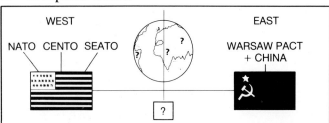

Many Third World countries in South America, Africa and Asia were nonaligned: that is, not under direct influence from West or East

14 The Thaw

My father died a terrible death. For the last twelve hours the lack of oxygen was acute. His face became dark. His lips were black. He literally choked to death as we watched.

In 1953 Stalin died. In Russia, and in the Communist countries of Eastern Europe, millions heaved a sigh of relief. Now people began to ask who would follow Stalin. What would be his attitude to the satellites of Eastern Europe? To America? To Communist China? How would US President Eisenhower react? After all, the Americans saw Stalin as a main reason for the development of the Cold War.

By 1953 the Cold War rules had changed. Each side could now destroy the other with H-bombs. Was this a chance for a thaw in the icy temperature of the Cold War? President Eisenhower hoped so. In April he said:

The new Soviet leadership has a precious opportunity to help turn the tide of history . . . we welcome every act of peace. (A)

But America's Secretary of State, John Foster Dulles, saw the Cold War differently (see **B**).

For two years Russia seemed to have several leaders. In 1955 Nikita Khruschev emerged as a clear leader. Khruschev was totally unlike the sinister Stalin. He loved to travel, and show off Russia's achievements. His personality seemed to offer a chance for better East–West relations. How was such an improvement to come about? Winston Churchill, Britain's Prime Minister, thought a conference at the highest level (a *summit*) should take place between the leading powers.

there might be a general feeling that they might do better than tear the human race, including themselves, to bits . . . (C)

B Dulles' ideas

Containment – America should encircle the USSR with countries friendly to America.

Massive retaliation – the Korean War taught America that next time she should fight Communism with a massive nuclear attack on the USSR.

Roll back – America should help the peoples of Eastern Europe, if they revolted against the control of the Russian Communists.

Khruschev liked the idea of a Summit Conference between the leaders of America, China, Britain, France and Russia. A meeting was arranged for July 1955 in Geneva, Switzerland. Hopes ran high in Europe. In fact little was agreed at Geneva, but at least the Great Powers met on friendly terms. The Russians said later 'it was a turning point in the relations between the Soviet Union and the West'.

A year later, in 1956, Khruschev told a meeting of top Communists that Stalin had been a bad and cruel leader. He also commented on Russia's dealings with the rest of the world:

There are only two ways: either peaceful co-existence, or the most destructive war in history. There is no third way. (D)

Behind Khruschev's idea of *peaceful co-existence* lay the basic idea that war between East and West did not have to happen. Khruschev was telling his audience three things: that in the age of H-bombs the ideas of Marx and Lenin were out-of-date and dangerous; that Russia should live peaceably with America, even if the two powers did not like one another; that Russia should work for Communist revolutions in other countries through peaceful means.

For the Russian satellite countries of Eastern Europe 'peaceful co-existence' looked promising. Under Stalin's rule they had been tied to Moscow. Now Khruschev's ideas suggested that the Russian view of Communism was not the only path the satellites could take. Khruschev himself spoke of 'different roads to Socialism'. Was Moscow's vice-like grip on the satellites over? Millions of Poles, Czechs and Hungarians hoped so.

?????????????????

1 How did Khruschev react to the idea of a summit meeting?

2 What were Khruschev's 'two ways' for Russia (**D**)?

3 a Explain in your own words what Khruschev meant by 'peaceful co-existence' (**D**).
b How did he think this would help the Communist cause in Russia and the rest of the world?
c Why did Khruschev's ideas give hope to many Eastern Europeans?

15 A Satellite Revolts

B During the revolt in Budapest a huge statue of Stalin was toppled to the ground and dragged through the streets

In 1956 Premier Khruschev's speech attacking Stalin's leadership sent shock waves through Russian satellites in Eastern Europe.

Stalin had treated East Germany, Poland and Hungary almost as 'slave colonies' of Russia. Hungary had to pay war reparations in food and goods to Russia. The standard of living in Eastern Europe got steadily worse; shortages of food were common. Workers in farms and factories were told to work harder for less. Each satellite had a feared secret police, prisons and labour camps. In Hungary alone 25 000 people had been executed without trial since 1945. Stalin-style Communism in Eastern Europe had left the people downtrodden and angry. In 1955 the satellites had been forced to sign the Warsaw Pact, binding them to Russia still further.

Now, with Khruschev's speech, people in the satellite countries saw new hope. They wanted three things: a higher standard of living; less direction from Russia in economic life and more political freedom from Russia. Each satellite wanted to develop a Communist society in its own way.

How would Russia react to these ideas? Although, Khruschev had begun the process of *De-Stalinisation*, would Russia allow her satellites to make changes? How would the West react if any changes were allowed?

Unrest began in Poland. In July 1956 a revolt against harsh living and working conditions broke out. Khruschev flew to Poland. He told the people:

❛*We have shed our blood to liberate this country and now you want to hand it over to the Americans.*❜ **(A)**

The revolt was settled by Russia granting the Poles some reforms. News of the Polish revolt spread to Budapest in Hungary. **B** shows what happened there. George Mikes was an eye-witness:

❛*Tempers were running high. A few thousand people went to the city park and surrounded the gigantic statue of Stalin. They got a rope round the neck and began to pull it . . . then it toppled slowly forward – laughter and applause greeted the symbolic fall of the former tyrant.*❜ **(C)**

Later the statue was dragged through the streets by a dustcart.

The protest gathered strength. Protesters and security police clashed at a radio station. Russian tanks rolled into the city. A battle developed:

❛*Every street was smashed – paving stones had been torn up, the streets were littered with burnt-out cars. I counted the carcasses of 40 Soviet tanks. Two monster Russian T.34 (tanks) lumbered past, dragging bodies behind them . . . a warning of what happened to freedom fighters.*❜ **(D)**

Street fighting raged on for five days. The Hungarian rebels were backed by the Hungarian Army. Only the security police stayed loyal to the Russians. Hundreds of police were lynched by the rebels.

The Russians were not strong enough to crush the

revolt. After talks with Imre Nagy, the new Hungarian Prime Minister, the Russian tanks pulled out of Budapest. The rebels went wild with delight.

Was Russia going to allow a satellite to defeat the Red Army? As news of the revolt came out of Hungary, what would the other Great Powers do?

In America, President Eisenhower said: 'I feel with the Hungarian people.' Secretary of State John Foster Dulles congratulated the Hungarians for challenging the Red Army. Earlier, Dulles had spoken of 'rolling back' Communism in Eastern Europe:

To all those suffering under Communist slavery, let us say: you can count on us. (E)

American radio stations in West Germany broadcast propaganda in support of the Hungarians. Many Hungarians believed that America would help them in their struggle against Moscow. But was America willing to run the risk of war to help the Hungarians?

On 1 November 1956 the Hungarians demanded far-reaching reforms. They wanted an end to the one-party system, and free elections. Hungary was to withdraw from the Warsaw Pact and to become a neutral, independent country.

This was too much for the Russians. They were afraid the iron curtain would be torn. Free elections might mean the end of Communism in Hungary. Other satellites might follow suit – that would be the end of Russia's buffer zone against the West.

Khruschev sought advice on what to do, from the Chinese Communists. His decision was made easier by world events. America was facing a presidential election. America was angry with Britain and France over their invasion of Egypt (see pages 51–53). World attention had moved to the Middle East, away from Eastern Europe.

On 4 November 1956, 6000 Russian tanks rumbled into Hungary. Bitter street fighting followed (**F**). George Mikes reported:

We have almost no weapons. People are running up to the tanks, throwing in hand-grenades and closing the windows. The Hungarian people are not afraid of death. We have just heard a rumour that American troops will get here within an hour or two. (G)

Desperate radio appeals were broadcast –

Civilised peoples of the world! Our ship is sinking. Light is fading. The shadows grow darker over the soil of Hungary. Extend us your aid. (H)

No aid came, only sympathy. 30 000 Hungarians were killed. 180 000 fled to the West through Austria. Nagy was imprisoned and later shot. A new Soviet-backed government was installed.

By 14 November the fighting was over. The American *Time Magazine* reported

The steel-shod Russian jackboot heeled down on Hungary this week, stamping and grinding out the young democracy. (J)

F Russian tanks after rioting in Budapest

??????????????

1 a Why did Hungary revolt against Russia in October 1956?
b How did the Hungarian revolt 'call the bluff' of: Russia's 'De-Stalinisation' policy; America's 'roll-back' idea?

2 *Either*
a Imagine you are a Hungarian rebel taking part in the scenes in **B** and **C** *or*
b Imagine you are a Russian tank commander during **F** and **G**.

Write about what you heard, saw and felt: during the events; an hour after the events took place.

3 *'In his attempts at reform Khruschev released forces beyond his control and one of his satellites almost broke away.'*   (*The Cold War*, Hastings)
Comment on this statement.

16 Love Story: Cold War Style

1959. Leonore Heinz was 31 and lonely. She lived in a large block of flats in Bonn, West Germany. By day she worked as a secretary in the Foreign Ministry of the West German Government.

One evening the doorbell rang. Outside stood a handsome man, clutching a bunch of red roses.

'Fraulein Newmann?' Leonore knew no-one of that name.

'No, I'm sorry. Have you got the right address?' The man checked a piece of paper, apologised and turned to go. Then a thought struck him.

'Here, you have these for the trouble I've caused you.'

Leonore was pleasantly surprised. She invited the man into her flat while she put the flowers in water. He introduced himself as Heinz Sutterlin, a freelance photographer. Over coffee they chatted and found they had many things in common. Heinz invited Leonore out to dinner a few nights later.

The months passed. Leonore saw more and more of Heinz. He showered her with dinner dates, gifts, concert tickets and visits. In December 1960 Heinz and Leonore were married. They decided that Leonore should keep up her job, since Heinz's income was unreliable.

One day Sutterlin asked Leonore to bring home some papers from her work. She was shocked and refused. Heinz insisted. What was Leonore to do? She was torn between her feelings of guilt, her love for Heinz and her fear of losing him. At last she gave in.

A   Heinz Sutterlin on his way to court to be tried for spying

Each lunchtime Leonore brought home papers in her handbag. While she cooked lunch, Heinz photographed the documents. In the afternoon Leonore returned them. No-one ever knew. In five years Sutterlin passed 3000 Foreign Ministry documents – a third of them secret – to his contact or case officer, a man called Runge.

Runge was an agent for the Russian spying organisation, the KGB, which was based in Moscow. He had worked undercover in West Germany for many years.

All went well for Heinz and Leonore until 1967. Then unknown to them Runge switched sides. He gave the names of all his agents in West Germany to America's spying organisation, the CIA (Central Intelligence Agency). Heinz and Leonore were arrested by the West German authorities (see **A**) and put on trial for spying.

At the trial it became clear that Sutterlin had trained as a spy for the East German Ministry of State Security. In 1959 he was taken over by Runge, who ordered him to marry a secretary from the West German Foreign Ministry.

Leonore was heartbroken when she realised that their romance and marriage had all been part of a Soviet KGB plan. Three weeks later, unable to live with the truth, Leonore committed suicide in her cell. She hanged herself with her nightdress.

Leonore Sutterlin was just one victim of the shadowy, undercover world of spying. The importance of the Sutterlins' work to the KGB was made clear by Runge:

'*We read official reports from abroad, even before the West German Foreign Minister.*' (B)

Winston Churchill described the world of spying as the 'Battle of the Conjurors' – a war between experts in deception. From the start of the Cold War there was a massive growth in spying operations (**C**). It became vital for each side to know what the other was doing, or thinking of doing.

The Sutterlin story shows up the three main features of Great Power spying operations. First, gathering information from a potential enemy. For the most part, the collection of KGB intelligence data from the West German Foreign ministry was a routine matter. Once obtained by Leonore (the sub-agent) and Heinz (the principal agent), the information was passed on by Runge to his superiors. Finally, it would be studied by KGB officers who were experts in West German affairs.

The second feature is that of counter-intelligence. Both the CIA and the KGB try to protect the secrecy of their agents and the work they are doing. Sometimes false information is deliberately leaked to confuse the

C Superpower spying organisations

America	The CIA was set up by President Truman in 1947 to '*perform . . . functions and duties relating to intelligence affecting the national security.*' Today the CIA has over 12 000 intelligence officers with about 4000 agents active in foreign countries.
Russia	The KGB came into being after Stalin's death in 1953. It developed from Stalin's feared secret police. The KGB employs 25 000 people on gathering intelligence from foreign countries. It operates 3000 to 5000 agents in over 90 different countries.

opposition. Each side goes to great lengths to gain information about the other's intelligence activities. In the case of the Sutterlins the CIA were only able to find out what they were doing when the KGB agent, Runge, changed sides.

The Sutterlin story also includes the third feature of Great Power spying. That is *covert operations* – interfering in the politics of other countries. The American and Russian governments use their intelligence agencies to support the governments of friendly countries and to put pressure on unfriendly ones. Cash aid, arms supplies, propaganda and spy training are some of the common forms of support or pressure.

For example in the 1950s the CIA were responsible for the overthrow of governments unfriendly to America in sensitive areas of American interest, such as Iran in the Middle East, and Guatemala in Latin America.

As both Great Powers developed their world-wide influence and interests, their spying operations grew. One incident, in 1960, was to show how far spying had come since the Cold War began, as the following section explains.

??????????????

1 a What false identity did Heinz use?
  b How did Heinz become a spy?
  c How long did Heinz and Leonore operate for?
  d Why did Leonore become a spy?
  e What sort of information do you think Leonore may have passed to Heinz?

2 a What is the Soviet spying organisation called?
  b What is the American spying organisation called?

3 Why do the Great Powers spend so much time and trouble spying on each other?

17 A Spy and a Summit

January 1960. A new decade dawned. Hopes of real progress in relations between America and Russia seemed possible. Both countries hoped that Russia's new spirit of co-operation could be built upon. In China, Premier Khruschev's ideas of peaceful co-existence were frowned upon. Relations between Russia and China were tense.

Peshawar, Pakistan, 1 May 1960. An American pilot, Gary Powers, takes off from his base. He is flying a Lockheed U2. It is a long-range, high-altitude spy plane. **A** shows his flight plan. Powers' mission is to take photographs of military sites in Russia. He is working for the CIA. The U2 is armed and the flight is dangerous. But America has been flying such missions for four years. Each one has been a success.

The flight goes well; the U2 photographs sites deep in Russia. Then disaster strikes. Flying at 68 000 feet above the Ural Mountains the aircraft is suddenly hit. Powers loses control as the U2 dives earthwards. He ejects from the aircraft and parachutes to the ground. The U2 crashes near Sverdlovsk. Four days later Premier Khruschev announces the news that an American plane has been shot down over Russia. No details are given. What was America to think? What should they say? Look at **B**.

On 7 May NASA (National Aeronautics and Space Administration: the US space research establishment) announced that a U2 research plane used 'to study weather conditions at high altitude' had been missing since 1 May when its pilot 'reported that he was having oxygen difficulties over Lake Van, Turkey area'. The same day the American Government said

there was no deliberate attempt to violate (fly into) *Soviet air space and never has been.* **(C)**

America denied that spy flights over Russia happened. America asked Russia for more information.

On 7 May Khruschev announced the full facts. The U2 had been shot down by a Soviet missile. Gary Powers had been captured 'alive and well'. He had admitted that he was on a spying mission. On his person were a poison pen and a silent pistol. Film taken on the U2's flight had been developed (**D**).

Russia had concrete proof. Not only had America been caught spying, but the American Government had also lied about the U2 flight. What hope had the Paris summit meeting – only days away? What would Khruschev do? How would Eisenhower react?

A The flight plan of the U2 spy plane

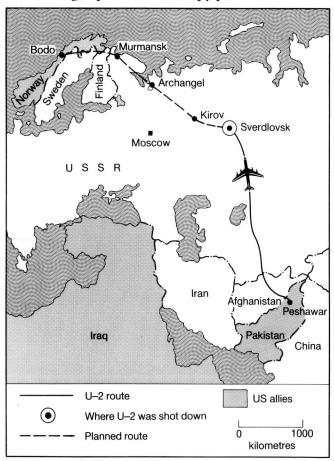

—— U–2 route	▨ US allies
⊙ Where U–2 was shot down	
– – – Planned route	0 1000 kilometres

B Questions and answers

These were the 'unknown elements' in the U2 case:

- Was the U2 really shot down? If so, by what: an aircraft; a missile?
- Was the aircraft totally destroyed? (It had a self-destruct unit.)
- Did the Russians find the U2's secret spying devices?
- Was Gary Powers dead?
- Did the Russians know that such flights had been going on for four years?

These were the ways America could answer Russia:

- Deny that the U2 was over Russian airspace
- Deny that the U2 was a spy plane
- Admit that the U2 must have strayed over Russian territory by mistake
- Admit that U2 spy flights took place over Russia
- Admit that U2s were over Russia, but for peaceful reasons, eg weather recording.

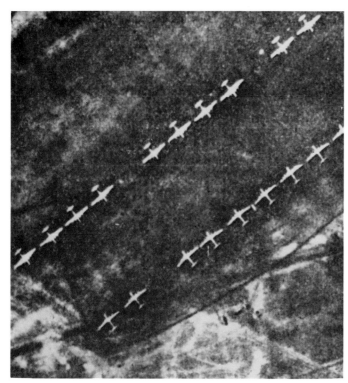

D   A Russian military airfield allegedly photographed by Gary Powers on his U2 spying mission

F   A newspaper cartoon from 1960. How would the U2 incident affect the Paris summit talks?

Faced with the evidence, America had to admit to a spying operation:

‹aircraft have made flights along the frontier of the free world for the past four years.› (E)

Khruschev demanded a full apology from America. The future of the summit talks lay on a knife edge (F). Khruschev was still prepared for the summit meeting to go ahead, providing Eisenhower admitted that the CIA made the U2 flights without his permission. This he would not do. Eisenhower said the flights were 'a vital necessity'.

As the leaders made their way to Paris, the U2 incident was still hot news. One day before the summit Khruschev listed his demands to America:

● America must apologise for the U2 affair.
● America must stop flights in the future.
● America must punish those responsible.

Eisenhower refused to apologise. The Paris Summit ended in uproar. Khruschev stormed out in anger and returned to Moscow. The U2 incident made Eisenhower very unpopular. Khruschev cancelled an invitation for Eisenhower to visit Russia. Russia condemned America's action at the UN.

Gary Powers was put on trial in Moscow and sentenced to ten years imprisonment. (He was released in 1962 in exchange for a Russian master spy.) American forces went on world-wide alert straight after the summit. Many people felt that America had ruined progress in East–West relations, and had threatened world peace. China thought that the U2 incident confirmed its view that Khruschev's idea of peaceful co-existence was wrong. America could never be trusted.

The 'thaw' was over. The icy chill of the Cold War days returned to relations between America and Russia. The world looked anxiously at areas of East–West tension, especially at an old sore – Berlin.

??????????????????

1 Look at **B**:
a Rank the 'unknown elements' in your order of importance for the Americans.
b What would you have advised the Americans to say to Russia?
c What did the Americans actually say?

2 What can you see in photograph **D**? Do you think this is convincing proof about the U2 spying mission? What makes you think so?

3 a What point is cartoon **F** making?
b What symbol of peace is shown in the cartoon?
c Do you think this is a Western or a Communist view of the U2 incident? Why?

4 Explain what effect the U2 incident had on relations between the Great Powers in 1960 (America/Russia; Russia/China; China/America). Did the incident mean the end of the 'thaw'?

18 Crisis in Berlin

Geneva, 1955. At a dinner party Nikita Khruschev rounds on the French Foreign Minister

'We shall never, never, never change our minds about the German problem. We shall never change our policy.' **(A)**

Tom Barman, a BBC foreign reporter, witnessed this scene.

'He left the room in silence. I believe he was genuine. It seems to me that the West . . . have not paid enough attention to the deep scars left on the Russian people by their appalling sufferings in two World Wars. The famine . . . slaughter and destruction . . . . are still fresh in their minds.' **(B)**

At the centre of 'the German problem' lay Berlin.

For ten years after the Berlin airlift (see page 11) the city returned to 'normal life'. 'Normal' that is, for Berlin. It stayed a divided city – in a divided nation. Berliners crossed sector boundaries for work and pleasure. Some, called *defectors*, crossed from East to West, never to return. The city was a gaping hole in the iron curtain.

In 1958 Khruschev tried to create a crisis over Berlin. He threatened to hand over the Western access routes into West Berlin to East Germany, and told the occupying armies to withdraw from patrolling Berlin. This led to a war of nerves between East and West. Though, in the end, Khruschev backed down, the Berliners stayed tense. Defections increased to 20 000 a month.

C Defectors from East to West Germany 1949–64

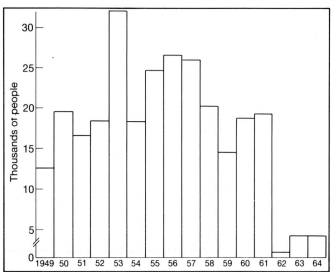

West and East Berlin were quite different. West Berlin recovered quickly from World War II. Thanks to American and West German aid, West Berlin throbbed with life. Its department stores bulged with consumer goods. In contrast the streets and shops of East Berlin were drab; consumer goods were difficult to buy.

This contrast was clear to Otto Seidel. He lived in East Germany but visited relatives in West Germany. Otto was a skilled engineer. At work he was fed-up with the ever-higher work targets. At home, supplies of meat and vegetables were in short supply. In May 1961, Otto and his family defected to a refugee centre in West Berlin. Over 2 million East Germans did the same **(C)**. This *exodus* (mass escape) was a serious and embarrassing problem. East Germany and Russia had to do something. The hole in the iron curtain had to be filled. On 3 August the Russian Government voiced its fears:

'Before everyone's eyes West Germany is becoming a seat of war danger in Europe. A regular army headed by former Hitler generals has sprung up there. Today West Germany has the largest army on the European continent among the NATO member countries.' **(D)**

The East German Government, under Russia's direction, acted. Police Sergeant Hans Peters and Ursula Heinemann were eye-witnesses to the events of 13 August 1961 in Berlin.

Hans was on border duty in the French Sector of West Berlin at the Strelitzer Strasse. At 2.20 am six trucks roared towards him, headlights blazing. 80 yards away they stopped. A moment later the street was full of armed soldiers who set up machine guns aimed at the French Sector. Two guards approached carrying coils of barbed wire. At the invisible border line between the Russian and French Sectors the squads cordoned off the street. In the houses of Strelitzer Strasse no-one stirred.

At 4.45 am Ursula Heinemann awoke in her East Berlin flat to another working day at the Plaza Hotel in West Berlin. She walked to the nearby station and went to the ticket counter. 'Nein! Nein! Take your pfennigs back! It's all over now with trips to Berlin.'

At that moment Ursula saw five armed East German transport police heading her way. She turned and ran back to her flat. 'They've closed the border!' In a moment the landing and corridors of the flats were full of people shouting and crying.

By early morning East German police and soldiers

G East German workers putting the 'finishing touches' to the Berlin Wall

had cut the city in two. Only a few crossing points stayed open, protected by tanks, armoured cars and water cannon. In the morning of 13 August, East German Radio broadcast that:

❛Measures have been taken . . . in the interests of peace in Europe and of the security of the GDR (East Germany) *and other Socialist states.❜* (**E**)

What would the West do? Worried West Berliners looked to America. America's new President, John F. Kennedy, wanted to show them support. Vice-President Johnson flew to Berlin. America protested to Russia about their action – but no more. Kennedy was not willing to risk war over Berlin.

❛The crisis is over. If the Russians wanted to attack us and cut off the access routes, they wouldn't be putting up barbed wire borders . . . I'm not going to get het up about it.❜ (**F**)

H An East German soldier leaps over the barbed wire at a Berlin border post to defect to the West, in 1961

The seal-off operation went on. Ursula Heinemann felt trapped. She decided that she must cross to the West. But how? Near the US Sector she slipped through an orchard and reached the barbed wire border. Ursula crawled forward on her stomach. She felt the metal barbs tearing her skin. At last she reached a border post. A moment later she was in West Berlin.

On 17 August the barbed wire began to be replaced with stone (**G**). The Berlin Wall had begun. Where houses formed the border, their windows were bricked up. Once the wall was finished, the East–West border was sealed. Many families and friends were forced to live apart.

The wall succeeded in stopping the flood of defectors to the West. 41 Germans were killed crossing the wall in its first year. But some were still determined to find ways of crossing from East to West (**H**).

??????????????

1 a Why did the West give West Berlin massive aid after World War II?
b In what way was a rich West Berlin a good 'advertisement for capitalism'?

2 Describe how the Seidel family might feel:
a six months before their defection;
b on the night of their defection;
c on the day after their defection;
d on the day after the Berlin Wall was built.

3 How did the building of the Berlin Wall affect: the people of East and West Berlin; relations between East and West in Europe?

19 Defector!

1962. The Berlin Wall has just been built. You wish to defect from East to West Berlin. You decide to build a tunnel under the Wall.

1 Where should the tunnel be built? Look at **A**: **a**, **b** and **c** are the best sites to start. Copy the map. Mark on it the site you have chosen and the planned route of the tunnel.

2 Who will help you build the tunnel? What type of people do you want? You have to trust them not to betray your plans. What questions will you ask them?

3 How are you going to pay for building the tunnel? It will cost about 50 000 marks (£4500). One way could be to sell the story to a West German magazine.

4 You begin to dig the tunnel. Use **C** to work out your progress. Toss a coin to find out what happens in each round. If it lands 'heads' upwards you make good progress. If it lands 'tails' up, you have a setback.

5 Write a diary recording what happens in each round. Copy map **B**, and shade in your progress on it.

6 After ten rounds your tunnel is finished. You dig up to the surface. Draw a line on your map to show where the tunnel comes up.

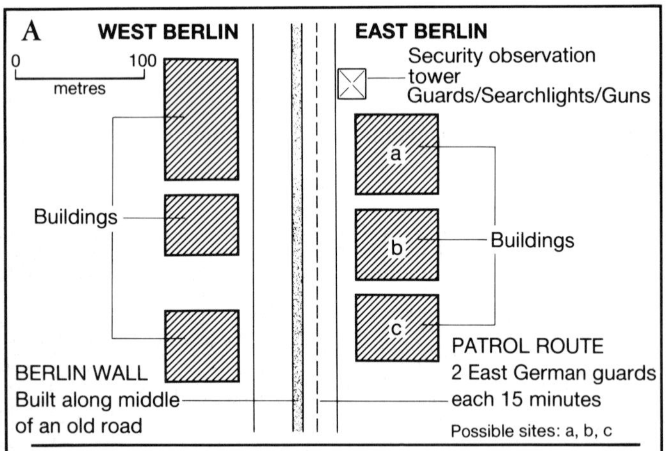

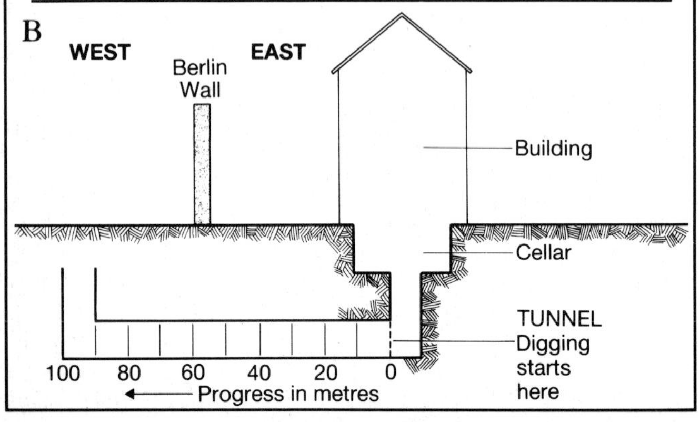

7 Is the tunnel in the right place? If it comes up in *East* Germany you have failed to escape. Write *Failure* on your map. If it comes up in the *West*, toss a coin:

Tails: The tunnel stops within range of the East German guards. It is too risky. You cannot use it. You have *failed.*
Heads: The tunnel comes up inside a West German building. You make last-minute escape plans. Go on to Stage 8.

8 The day arrives. You and the other defectors meet up at the entrance to the tunnel. Toss a coin:

Tails: One of the defectors has betrayed the plan to the East German police! They arrest all of you and destroy the tunnel. You have *failed.*
Heads: You all struggle through the tunnel. You come up in West Germany. You give yourselves up to the police. You have *succeeded* in defecting to the West.

9 Record the result of your attempt in your diary. How do you feel about your:
Success: happy, relieved, hopeful, sad . . .?
Failure: disappointed, frightened, determined . . .?

C

Round	Progress (**T** = tails; **H** = heads)
1	**H** Digging goes well. 10 metres dug.
	T Shortage of wood for roof and wall supports. 5 metres dug.
2	**H** You find a supply of wood. 20 metres dug.
	T Difficult soil conditions slow down work. 10 metres dug.
3	**H** You sell tunnel story to West German magazine for 30 000 marks.
	T Funds for tunnel run low.
4	**H** You dig in shifts, day and night. 20 metres dug.
	T Digging cracks water pipe. Tunnel floods. No progress.
5	**H** Work goes well. 15 metres dug.
	T Removing loose soil slows down work. 5 metres dug.
6	**H** You build wheeled trolley for soil removal. 15 metres dug.
	T Stale air makes digging difficult. 5 metres dug.
7	**H** Fresh air pump fitted. 10 metres dug.
	T Border guards use sound detectors.
8	**H** You select last of defectors. All agree to pay 5000 marks.
	T Rumour of security leak to East German police. No work in tunnel.
9	**H** Digging goes well. 20 metres dug.
	T Roof-top guards make digging difficult. 10 metres dug.
10	**H** Digging goes well. 15 metres dug.
	T Your tunnel hits earlier tunnel. Roof caves in.

A

WEST BERLIN | **EAST BERLIN**
Security observation tower
Guards/Searchlights/Guns
0 — 100 metres
Buildings
a
b
c
Buildings
BERLIN WALL
Built along middle of an old road
PATROL ROUTE
2 East German guards each 15 minutes
Possible sites: a, b, c

B

WEST | **EAST**
Berlin Wall
Building
Cellar
TUNNEL
Digging starts here
100 80 60 40 20 0
← Progress in metres

20 The Berlin Wall: Propaganda

A is an example of propaganda. This cartoon appeared in a West German magazine. It shows the leader of East Germany announcing 'total state security' by evacuating the whole population to China!

Throughout the Cold War both sides made great use of propaganda. The war of words became an important weapon. Each Great Power used propaganda to support its own political system and to attack the other's. The capitalist West attacked Communism. The Communist East attacked capitalism. Every form of mass-media – radio, books, newspapers, posters, film, and speeches – has been used. Each side makes use of propaganda to present its view of events and Great Power motives.

The Berlin Wall was a *visible* sign of East–West hostility, and both sides used it as a source for a stream of propaganda. **B–F** are all examples of this. For each, decide which side – East or West – has produced the propaganda.

The frontiers of our republic will be protected at all cost. We

A Cartoons are used by both sides in the 'propaganda war' between East and West

will do everything to stop the criminal activities of Western Germany and the American spies. **(B)**

A great city has been slashed in two by a big ugly barrier eight feet high. At regular intervals are watch towers manned by policemen with machine guns, on the look out for anyone trying to escape what is now, visibly, the huge penitentiary (prison) of the Soviet zone. **(C)**

The Western powers in West Berlin use it as a centre of subversive activity (action to undermine a government) *against the GDR. In no other part of the world are so many espionage centres to be found. These centres smuggle their agents into the GDR for all kinds of subversion: recruiting spies; sabotage; provoking disturbances . . .*

The government addresses all working people of the GDR with a proposal that will securely block subversive activity so that reliable safeguards and effective control will be established around West Berlin, including its border with democratic Berlin. **(D)**

All free men, wherever they may be are citizens of Berlin, and thus I take pride in saying 'Ich bin ein Berliner' (I am a Berliner). **(E)**

When the border with West Berlin was closed . . . for the first time the GDR was able to begin building up a socialist state within sabotage-proof borders. **(F)**

??????????????

1 What point is the cartoonist of **A** trying to make?

2 What basic reason for building the Wall do **B**, **D** and **F** all agree on?

3 What reason does **D** give for building the Berlin Wall? What reason might a non-Communist give?

4 **E** was spoken by US President Kennedy. How do you think: Communists/non-Communists would have reacted to this speech?

5 What reason does **F** give for East Germany's economic problems? What reason might a non-Communist give?

6 Design a poster for either West Berlin or East Berlin about the Berlin Wall. Use the drawing itself, the slogan and the caption to show a deliberately one-sided view of the Wall. (Use the information on pages 30–31 to help you.)

21 Missile Crisis!

This is a decision-making activity about the Cuban missile crisis. It will help you think about some of the complex factors involved in negotiations between the Great Powers. When you have finished, turn to page 38 to find out what *actually* happened.

THE AMERICAN VIEW

Since 1933, Cuba had been run by a pro-American dictator called Fulgencio Batista. America had helped him stay in power. America had helped Cuba's trade and bought most of its main crop – sugar cane. Americans had owned most of the land and industries.

In 1959 Batista was overthrown in a revolution led by Fidel Castro. Castro was a Marxist and unpopular with America. America refused to lend Castro any money. Castro wanted to end US control of Cuba and distribute land to the poor. He began to take over much of the land and wealth owned by Americans. America refused to buy Cuban sugar, but Russia agreed to buy it from Cuba. Castro and Chairman Khruschev became friends. Now America had a Communist neighbour only 90 miles from her mainland! The Cubans allowed the Russians to build bases on Cuba.

In 1961 followers of Batista, with limited American support, tried to overthrow Castro. The force landed at the Bay of Pigs, but it was defeated. Castro's policies became more anti-American. A Communist Cuba, backed by Russia, was a threat to American security!

President Kennedy   Elected in 1960, Kennedy was the youngest President in American history. He was full of ideals, charming and active. Many Americans looked forward to a new era of progress under Kennedy. Kennedy took over some old problems – like Berlin, and some new ones – like Cuba. He knew the Bay of Pigs attempt had been a mistake. Kennedy was determined to make America strong and safe and to defend free countries from Communism. Kennedy wished to avoid nuclear war with Russia if at all possible.

Chairman Khruschev   Khruschev had cleverly become the sole leader of the USSR and had attacked Stalin's policies. Khruschev was keen on 'peaceful co-existence' with America; this seemed to offer hope. But Khruschev was an unpredictable leader – he could be friendly but also brutal as over the Berlin Wall issue. He wanted to be seen as a strong leader of the

Communist World. Khruschev was proud of Russia's strength.

THE RUSSIAN VIEW

Since 1933 Cuba had been run by a corrupt and violent dictator called Batista. He was supported in power by America. The USA dominated Cuba's trade and bought most of its main crop – sugar. America exploited the Cubans – owning the best land and biggest industries. There was a wide gulf between the rich and poor.

In 1959 Batista was overthrown by a 'people's revolution' led by Fidel Castro. America refused to assist Castro, even refusing to buy Cuba's sugar crop. Castro wanted to end America's exploitation of Cuba. He wanted a fair society based on Communist ideas: the first one in the Americas. America cut all ties with Cuba. The USSR stepped in to purchase Cuba's sugar and gave vast amounts of aid. Castro was grateful. He and Khruschev became friends.

In 1961 American land and air forces tried to invade Cuba and remove its legal government. Understandably, Castro looked to Russia for protection against the threat of further American attack. Russia was glad to defend Cuba with military equipment. To the Americans Russia's friendship with Cuba looked like a threat to their security.

President Kennedy   Kennedy was a new President. He had many problems to solve in America. In 1961 Chairman Khruschev had met President Kennedy at a summit meeting in Vienna. The young US President had not impressed Khruschev. Already he had made mistakes, such as the Bay of Pigs failure in 1961. Kennedy had done little to stop Khruschev building the Berlin Wall in 1961. Was Kennedy too young, too inexperienced to cope? Could Khruschev use this inexperience to Russian advantage?

Chairman Khruschev   Khruschev was at the height of his power. He had emerged as leader some years after Stalin's death. He had attacked Stalin and ended many of his policies. He was a clever leader who wished to protect Russia at all costs. Khruschev was keen on peaceful co-existence with America, but he wanted Russia to be strong to defend itself. Khruschev was worried about the US missile bases that ringed Russia. The USSR did not have bases close to the USA. Khruschev was a strong leader of the Communist World.

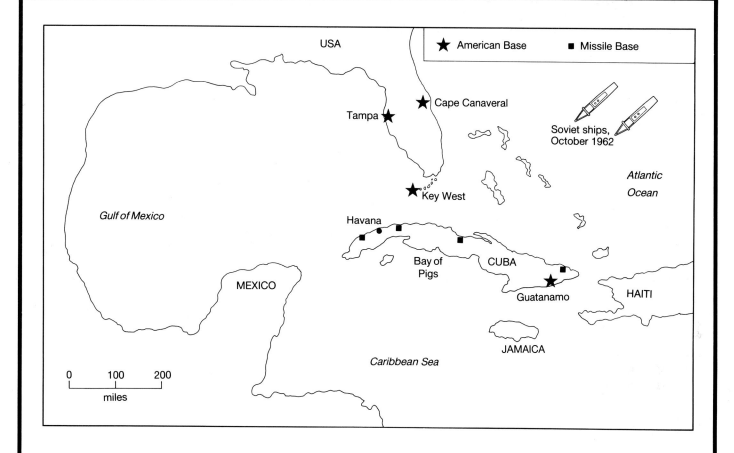

HOW TO PLAY

Divide into two sides: Russia and America. Choose a leader (Khruschev or Kennedy) and a team of advisors for each side. Using the evidence and information on this and the following pages, try to work out what action your side should take at each stage (1–6) as the crisis develops. Each side can communicate with the other through notes, telegrams or meetings.

Leaders

1 Read your side's view of the Cuban situation and the other side's leader.
2 Study the *Guidelines for action* and map **A**.
3 Use your advisors to help you decide what to do, and to help you negotiate with the other side.

Remember You bear the responsibility. Your decision is final.

Advisors

You represent the following
● Military – the chiefs of army, navy and airforce
● Diplomatic – experts in foreign affairs
● Political – supporters of the leader
● Intelligence – experts in how the other side thinks!

1 Read your side's view of the Cuban situation and the other side's leader.
2 Study the *Guidelines for action* and map **A**.
3 Concentrate on giving the leader your expert knowledge (you can also comment on other matters).

Remember If you cannot all agree what to do, your leader's decision is final.

GUIDELINES FOR ACTION

Read these through carefully

1 Always discuss *different options* at each stage of the events – do not just think of *one*.
2 Always discuss the *advantages* and *disadvantages* of what you are considering.
3 Always think about how the *other side* might *react* to your actions.
4 Always think about how far your side is prepared to go – and how far the other side might go.
5 Always try to choose a course of action which will give your side, and the other side, time to think.
6 Remember that, whatever happens, neither side will want to back down or 'lose face' in the eyes of the world.

ACTION

Stage 1, September 1962
CIA reports from Cuban refugees indicate a build-up of Russian bases on Cuba.

– The Americans receive the information first. The leader and advisors study it and discuss what to do. Then they inform Russia of America's action.

– Russia goes second. The leader and advisors study America's action and discuss how to react. They then inform America of Russia's reaction.

Follow this pattern for each stage of the crisis

Stage 2, 16 October 1962
An American U2 flies over Cuba and takes photograph **B**. The CIA identify missile sites being built for use with Russian nuclear missiles.

Stage 3, 17 October 1962
American Intelligence reports that the 16–32 missiles on Cuba could kill 80 million Americans in a range of 2000 miles (see map **C**). Their flight time is 17 minutes.

Stage 4
Over 20 Russian ships are spotted in mid-Atlantic, en route for Cuba. On board are missiles, in crates (**D**).

Stage 5, 25 October 1962
Further U2 photographs (**E**) show that work continues on missile bases on Cuba. The sites will be ready in a few days.

Stage 6, 27 October 1962
A U2 is shot down by a Russian missile over Cuba. The pilot is killed.

B   The first U2 photographs showed missile bases like this being built on Cuba

C   **American towns within range of missiles from Cuba**

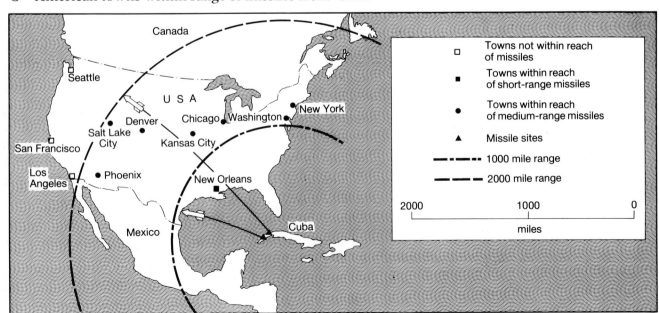

D A US Navy ship (in the foreground) alongside a Russian freighter loaded with missiles for Cuba

E Further U2 photographs showed details of the Cuban missile bases

22 The Cuban Crisis

In September 1962 America became worried about military bases on Cuba, its near neighbour. President Kennedy had warned Premier Khruschev not to put Soviet nuclear missiles on Cuba. Khruschev said he had no intention of doing so. Robert Kennedy, the President's brother, wrote:

❛Tuesday, 16 October 1962 *President Kennedy asked me to come to the White House . . . U2 reconnaissance had convinced* (the CIA) *that Russia was placing missiles and atomic weapons on Cuba.* ❜ (A)

Here was proof that the Russians had been lying! Some missiles were on Cuba. Others were on Russian ships in mid-Atlantic, heading for Cuba. America had to act.

So began the most serious crisis of the Cold War. It brought the USA and USSR to the brink of nuclear war, and humanity to the edge of extinction. Two men, President Kennedy and Premier Khruschev, would decide the fate of the human race.

Robert Kennedy was a member of a Committee of the National Security Council. This committee advised the President. They met daily at the White House, throughout the crisis. President Kennedy wanted to explore every possible course of action.

❛*It isn't the first step that concerns me, but both sides escalating to the fourth or fifth steps, and we don't go to the sixth because there is no one around to do so.* ❜ (B)

What was America's first step to be? **C** shows six possible options.

On 22 October President Kennedy announced his decision.

❛*I have directed that the following initial steps be taken: first, a strict 'quarantine' on all offensive military equipment under shipment to Cuba. All ships, if found to contain cargoes of offensive weapons, (will) be turned back.* ❜ (D)

The blockade began on 24 October. Cuba was ringed by 100 American warships. America made other military moves. Plans for an invasion of Cuba were drawn up. 52 bombers, armed with nuclear bombs, flew patrols. Rules for stopping and boarding the Russian ships were agreed between politicians and America's naval forces. America got support for its action from allies in South America and in Europe.

How would the Russians react to America's 'quarantine'. Would Americans really stop Russian ships or was America bluffing? The Soviet ships sailed on, escorted by a Russian submarine. Robert Kennedy remembers

C Cuban missile crisis: options and considerations

Option	Advantages	Disadvantages
Do nothing – allow missiles to be based in Cuba.	Gives time to prepare response.	Unpopular in America. Major success for USSR. Threat to US security.
Attack Cuba/USSR with nuclear weapons.	Strike first – before USSR attacks USA in same way.	Full-scale nuclear war, millions killed – the end of humanity?
Air strike against the Cuban missile bases.	Destroy missiles and sites already in Cuba.	War with Cuba and perhaps the USSR. No guarantee all sites would be destroyed.
Blockade Cuba with US Navy – no Russian ships allowed through.	Limited pressure – could be increased later. USSR would be forced to fire first shot to break blockade.	Missiles and sites in Cuba would not be affected. Conflict with USSR rather than Cuba. USSR might do the same to West Berlin.
Air attack against all military sites in Cuba.	Destroy missiles and sites already in Cuba.	Direct conflict with Cuba and perhaps USSR? US casualties.
Invasion of Cuba by US Armed Forces.	Destroy missiles and sites.	War with Cuba and perhaps USSR. US casualties (estimated 25 000). USSR might invade West Berlin.

what happened when the first ships reached the quarantine line

❛The minutes ticked slowly by. It was 10.25. A messenger brought in a note. 'Mr President, we have a report that some of the Russian ships have stopped dead in the water.' I looked at the clock – 10.32. Later the report came that the Russian ships closest to the barrier had stopped or had turned round.❜ (E)

Russia had pulled back from direct conflict but the crisis was not over. U2 photos showed that the missile sites on Cuba were nearly finished. Russian bombers were also being assembled. Within a week 80 million Americans could be killed from Cuba.

On Friday, 26 October, President Kennedy got a letter from Khruschev. In it, Russia offered to remove the missiles from Cuba if Kennedy promised not to invade Cuba and to end the blockade. Above all, Khruschev made it clear he wished to avoid the horror of nuclear war. The letter offered the first hope of a peaceful solution. But the next morning a second letter arrived from Khruschev. It took a harder line:

❛Our purpose has been to help Cuba develop as its people desire. You want to relieve your country from danger. Your rockets are stationed on Turkey. You are worried about Cuba. You say it worries you because it lies at a distance of 90 miles from the United States. Turkey lies next to us!

I make this proposal. We agree to remove from Cuba offensive means (nuclear missiles). The United States on its part, will remove its similar means from Turkey.❜ (F)

Kennedy was confused. Which of Khruschev's letters should he believe – the first or the second? How should America respond? Turkey was a NATO ally. Kennedy would not accept a 'trade-off' of Cuban missiles for Turkish missiles. But if America attacked Cuba, might Russia do the same to Turkey?

That day, a U2 pilot was killed. His aircraft was shot down over Cuba by a Russian missile. Robert Kennedy remembers:

❛There was a feeling that the noose was tightening. The President's mind went to other areas of the world. What was going to occur in Berlin, in Turkey, if we attacked Cuba? We were deciding really for all mankind.❜ (G)

What should America do?

❛There were arguments – sharp disagreements. Everyone was tense, some were near exhaustion – all were weighed down with worry. I suggested that we ignore the latest Khruschev letter and respond to his earlier letter's proposal.❜ (H)

President Kennedy took up his brother's idea. His reply accepted Khruschev's first 'offer'.

❛1 You agree to remove weapon systems from Cuba and to halt their further introduction into Cuba.

2 We agree a) to remove the quarantine measures now in effect. b) to give assurances against an invasion of Cuba.❜ (J)

If Russia had not responded by Monday, 29 October, America would invade Cuba. Was the world one day away from a Third World War?

Khruschev's reply came on 28 October. He accepted Kennedy's offer. The Cuban crisis was over. The world heaved a sigh of relief. On Cuba, within two months, no trace was left of the missiles of October.

K shows the lessons that America and Russia learnt as a result of the Cuban missile crisis.

K   Results of the crisis

- Alongside their power, America and Russia also had responsibilities towards the rest of the world.
- Brinkmanship (pushing each other to the brink of war) was too deadly a game to play.
- Moscow and Washington should be in closer and more direct contact – in 1963 a 'Hot line' teleprinter link was set up.
- Nuclear arms control talks should begin – in August 1963 a Test Ban Treaty was signed between America, Russia and Britain.
- Direct conflict between America and Russia, anywhere around the world, should be avoided.

??????????????

1 a What did President Kennedy mean by **B**?
b Which option in **C** would you have advised President Kennedy to choose? Why?
c Which option did President Kennedy actually choose? Why do you think he chose it?

2 a What did Khruschev mean by 'as its people desire' in **F**?
b Was Khruschev's proposal in **F** reasonable?

3 Why was President Kennedy deciding 'for all mankind' (**G**)?

4 Look at **K**.
a What is 'brinkmanship'?
b What was the 'Hot line'?
c Put the 'lessons' learned by America and Russia in your order of importance for helping to promote peace.

5 How well do you think President Kennedy handled America's response to events in Cuba, 1960–62? Give reasons for your answer.

23 Czechoslovakia 1968

A The invasion of Czechoslovakia

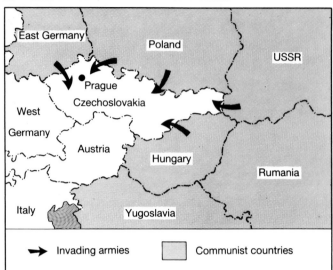

At midnight, 20 August 1968, Ladislav Mnacko awoke. He peered out of his window. What were those shadowy shapes standing in line all along Stefanik Street? Trucks? They couldn't be . . . the road was closed for repairs; nothing could be driven along it. Then he was sure. Tanks. Tanks can drive anywhere. A lot of tanks.

Czechoslovakia had been invaded (see map **A**). Why had Czechoslovakia's allies acted to crush a fellow Warsaw Pact member?

Since the spring of 1968 the Czech Prime Minister, Alexander Dubček had been trying to improve living conditions in Czechoslovakia:

❛We want to set new forces of Socialist life in motion in this country, allowing a fuller application of the advantages of Socialism.❜ (B)

Freedom of speech was introduced in newspapers, on the radio, and on television. Trade with the West was developed. Different religions were allowed. Dubček's Government, though still Communist, wished to take less control over people's lives. Dubček called his ideas *'Socialism with a human face'*. The people of Czechoslovakia gave him their full support. The thaw in Czech Communism in early 1968 was known as the 'Prague Spring'.

The Czechs tried very hard not to upset Russia. They remembered how Hungary had been crushed in 1956 (see pages 24–25). Czechoslovakia had no wish to make changes in its foreign affairs. It wished to stay a loyal ally of Russia in the Warsaw Pact.

But Dubček's changes were too much for Leonid Brezhnev, the Russian leader, and other Warsaw Pact leaders. They met, and warned Czechoslovakia not to run the risk of opening up a 'hole' in the iron curtain:

❛The word democracy is being misused. There are campaigns against honest Party workers. The aim is to end the leading role of the Party, to undermine Socialism and to turn Czechoslovakia against other Socialist countries. Thus . . . the security of our countries is threatened.❜ (C)

On 20 August the Warsaw Pact forces invaded Czechoslovakia with 400 000 troops.

Why was Russia so frightened of change in Czechoslovakia? The Czech historian, Zeman, gives a clue:

❛Twice in this century the Russians have had to face an onslaught from the centre of Europe. Only they know the extent of their losses in the last war . . . and the country is still governed by the men who fought in it. The Russians have no intention of dismantling their defences to the west.❜ (D)

The West was shocked by the invasion (see **E**). But would the West support Czechoslovakia – or do nothing, as in Hungary in 1956?

To avoid bloodshed, the Czechs decided to offer 'passive resistance'. The campaign was organised through radio station broadcasts, like **F**.

E Newspaper headlines from 21 August 1968, after the Russian invasion of Czechoslovakia

‘Citizens – go to work normally . . . keep calm . . . do not give the occupation forces any excuse for armed action . . . show the invaders your scorn in silence.’ **(F)**

As the Russians took control arrests of leading Czechs began.

The Russians tried to find the radio stations and close down their transmitters.

‘We do not know how long we will be able to broadcast. If you hear a new unknown voice on this station, do not believe it.’ **(G)**

The Russian troops were surprised to see how much the Czechs hated them **(H)**. They had believed Soviet propaganda:

‘Tass is authorized to state that the leaders of the Czechoslovak Socialist Republic have asked the Soviet Union and allied states to render the Czechoslovak people urgent assistance. This request was brought about by the threat which has arisen to the Socialist system, existing in Czechoslovakia.’ **(J)**

(*Tass*, 21 August 1968)

The Russian leader, Brezhnev, justified Russia's action:

‘When forces that are hostile to Socialism try to turn the development of some Socialist country towards capitalism . . . it becomes not only a problem of the country concerned, but a common problem and concern of all Socialist countries.’ **(K)**

Other satellites in Eastern Europe took careful note of this idea, which came to be known as 'the Brezhnev Doctrine'. Alexander Dubček was flown to Moscow. For days Czech and Russian leaders talked. On 27 August the Czech leaders returned from Moscow. The Czech President Ludvik Svoboda announced

‘Dear fellow citizens . . . after four days of negotiations in Moscow we are back with you. Neither you nor we felt at ease.’ **(L)**

Alexander Dubček:

‘to normalize the present complex situation . . . it will be necessary to take measures limiting freedom of expression as we have become accustomed to it.’ **(M)**

Russian troops were allowed to stay in Czechoslovakia. Censorship was brought back. The heavy hand of Moscow once more gripped Czechoslovakia. A Czech student, Jan Palach, set fire to himself in the centre of Prague as a protest. In April 1969 Dubček resigned. His idea of making Czechoslovakian Communism more human lay in ruins.

How would the other Great Powers react to Russia's action? China quickly condemned the Russian invasion.

H In Prague there were violent protests against the Russian invasion

This was a sign of the poor relations which existed between Russia and China (see pages 44/45). 12 years earlier, Russia had sought China's advice before invading Hungary. The West watched events with horror, but did nothing.

The invasion of Czechoslovakia came at a crucial time in the gradual building-up of links between America and Russia (see pages 56/57). America knew that serious action on behalf of the Czechs could set back the slow process of improving East–West relations. This they would not risk. In 1968 the Czechs were left to their fate by the West, as they had been at Munich 30 years earlier.

In January 1969 there were celebrations in Prague. The reason was ice-hockey. The Czechs recorded a rare win over the Russians! But in the power-play of politics, the Russians were the victors, the Czechs the victims, and the West the spectators.

??????????????

1 Explain what was meant by:
a the 'Prague Spring';
b passive resistance;
c the 'Brezhnev Doctrine'.

2 What does **H** suggest about the Czech reaction to the Russian invasion?

3 Why did Russia invade Czechoslovakia in 1968? (Think about: political reasons; strategic reasons.) What effect did Russia's action have on relations between Russia and China, and Russia and America?

B Russia provided China with the money and technology for massive building projects, like this bridge over the Yangtze River

The Korean War made East and West distrust each other even more. After it, the Cold War became a world-wide matter, rather than a European one. In the Far East, the East–West conflict was complicated. America faced the combined strength of the two Communist giants.

Before the Korean War, Russia and China had signed a Treaty of Friendship.

❛The USSR will give credits to China to the amount of 300 000 000 US dollars – used for payments for deliveries from the Soviet Union of equipment and materials (for electric power stations, engineering plants, mining equipment, railways and other transport equipment).❜ **(A)**   (14 February 1950)

Russian aid flooded into China after 1950. Russian experts masterminded China's first Five Year Plan. **B** shows a massive new bridge being built over the River Yangtze. It was one of over 200 industrial projects in China built by Russians. By the mid 1950s, 10 000 Russian experts were working in China and 10 000 Chinese were being trained in Russia. Half of China's trade was with Russia. Russia loaned China 2000 million dollars to help fight the Korean War. It seemed as if the two Communist giants were thinking and acting as one. Mao said of Russia:

❛We belong to the front headed by the Soviet Union.❜ **(C)**

In 1956 Khruschev sought Mao's advice before acting against Hungary. Khruschev warned America that

❛an attack on the Peoples' Republic of China is an attack on the Soviet Union.❜ **(D)**

The West had further cause for concern when, in 1957, Russia promised to supply China with nuclear weapons. Mao was certain that Russian missile strength, linked with China's manpower, would prove to be an unbeatable combination against America. Mao believed that nothing could stop the eventual spread of Communism.

After Korea, America lost no time in getting together friendly countries in South East Asia. With America's help they would defend the area in case of

Communist expansion. The result was SEATO (the South East Asia Treaty Organisation). America confirmed its support by signing a Peace Treaty with Japan. In February 1955 America signed a defence treaty with Nationalist China. An American fleet protected Formosa (Taiwan). Chiang Kaishek was kept in power with massive amounts of American aid, much to China's disgust.

America still saw Mao as a puppet of Russia, directed by Moscow. Over this, America badly misjudged the facts. Mao's Communism was a different brand to Moscow's. In South East Asia it was the Chinese version that posed the greatest threat to America.

America's response was to isolate China at the UN, through trade and politics. As a result, China turned more towards Russia. China did have a genuine wish to spread Communism throughout South East Asia. If necessary, this would be achieved by aggression (partly in response to the America threat). Mao had said:

violent Revolution is accomplished by the power of the gun. (**E**)

Mao's threats worried Americans. They saw the Chinese as a 'Yellow Peril', which would sweep across South East Asia, spreading revolution. America warned China that she would not be allowed to expand. When, in 1955, China tried to gain some off-shore islands, America threatened to use tactical nuclear weapons. The Chinese backed down. America's idea of *brinkmanship* (going to the brink of war to force the enemy to retreat) had paid off.

America's view of the countries of South East Asia was known as the 'domino theory' (**F**). If one 'domino' was allowed to fall to Communism, others would fall as well. As President Eisenhower said:

the loss of any single country in South East Asia could lead to the loss of all Asia, then India and Japan, finally endangering the security of Europe. (**G**)

America thought that Korea had been the first 'domino'. Only strong American action had held it upright.

China's leaders saw South East Asia in a different light. Although wanting Communism to triumph, China's leaders were realistic. The Vice Premier said:

If the countries are not ripe for revolution, then China can do nothing about it. China cannot turn revolutions on or off when she wants to. (**H**)

Nevertheless, the domino theory took root in American minds. America was determined to support South East Asia, whenever the dominoes were threatened.

F

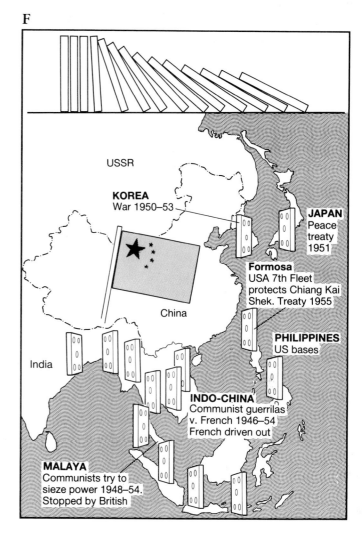

??????????????

1 a Why did Russia supply aid to China after 1949 (**A**)?
b What sort of aid did Russia send?

2 a How did America try to isolate China? What was the result of these attempts?
b Why might Mao's words in **E** worry America?
c How did America react to China's attempt to expand in 1955?

3 a Look at **F**. What steps did America take to contain the spread of Communism in South East Asia after 1953?
b Explain, in your own words, what the 'domino theory' was.
c Which country, in America's view, had been the first domino?

4 Does the Chinese view of Communist Revolution (**H**) suggest that America's fears were justified?

25 The Sino—Soviet Split

On 12 October 1954 China and Russia declared that:

❝*The friendly relations between the USSR and China will be the basis of close co-operation . . . . founded on the sincere desire to assist one another to strengthen ties of brotherly friendship.*❞ **(A)**

Cartoon **B** shows the 'two against one' situation that existed between the Great Powers in the 1950s. China and Russia seemed to be close friends. Russia was helping China to modernise her military forces, farming and factories.

China exploded her first H-bomb on 17 June 1967 **(C)**. In 1954 Russia had promised to help China develop nuclear weapons. But events since then had damaged the friendship. China had to develop her own nuclear arms. The Chinese leader, Mao Zedong, said:

❝*We are now in fourth place in the world. This is the result of Khruschev's 'help'. He forced us to take our own road. We should give him a big medal.*❞ **(D)**

China would never rely on Russia again. The two Communist giants seemed more like enemies than friends. What had caused the Sino (Chinese) – Soviet split?

Before Mao gained power in 1949 there had been disagreements. Mao thought Stalin had given him bad advice in the 1920s. He felt that Russia did not understand Chinese Communism, which, unlike that of Russia, was based on the support of the peasants. In the Chinese Civil War, Stalin gave Mao only lukewarm support against Chiang Kaishek.

After Mao came to power there was a 'honeymoon period' of friendship with Russia, which lasted until 1955 (see pages 14–15). Even then, there were problems.

B This cartoon shows China and Russia in league against the snarling tiger – America

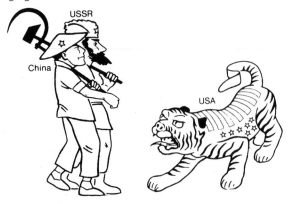

C The mushroom cloud created by the explosion of China's first hydrogen bomb

For example, Russia and China disagreed about farming. Russia wanted mechanised farming with few workers. The Chinese wanted *more* work for the millions of peasants, not less.

Another cause of tension was the Russian view of Mao and China. Stalin treated China as just another Soviet satellite, like Hungary or Poland. Mao respected Stalin, but he would not be Moscow's puppet. He was determined to take an independent line. But in order to modernise, China did need Russia's aid and advice.

In 1956, Khruschev's speech against Stalin sent shock waves to Peking. Mao disagreed with Khruschev in three ways. First, Mao thought that Stalin had been a good leader of the Communist world. Was Khruschev's attack on Stalin's leadership a sideways dig at the similar style of Mao in China? Second, China disagreed with Russia's idea that Communism could be achieved without revolution. To China, revolution and war were the ways to Communist success. Third, China thought that Khruschev's idea of peaceful co-existence was wrong. Was it not a betrayal of the ideas of Marx and Lenin, to seek any sort of friendly relations with the West, especially America?

Relations between China and Russia became more and more strained. In 1955, Mao objected to Russian offers of aid to Third World countries like India and Burma. Russia's refusal to help China's attack on offshore islands held by Chiang Kaishek angered the Chinese. In 1958 Russia condemned Mao's *Great Leap Forward* plan to modernise Chinese industry. Russia called the plan:

❛a road of dangerous experiment, a road of disregard for the experience of other socialist (Communist) states.❜ (E)

In 1960 Russia withdrew its aid and its technical experts from China. Half-finished factories were left to rust. Khruschev also tore up the agreement to share nuclear weapons with China. Military aid from Russia to China stopped. Trade between the two was affected (F).

The Western powers wondered what was going on. Anthony Lawrence, a BBC correspondent based in the Far East at the time, commented:

❛If it is true that the Soviet Union and China have started a real quarrel, then this is one of the great events of modern history . . . The main cause of disagreement seems to be in the minds of the Chinese leaders themselves. The legend is being fostered that the USA is on its last legs – a paper tiger – and that the triumph of the Communist world is imminent. They say that Khruschev has shown too soft an attitude and it's time the super-race – the Chinese – took over the leadership of the Communist camp.❜ (G)

In 1963 Mao made the split public. Each side poured out hostile propaganda – in speeches, radio broadcasts, posters and newspapers:

❛Throughout the past year scarcely a day has passed without Brezhnev and Kosygin attacking China's great revolution. A tragedy has taken place in international Communism. Its creators are the scabs – Khruschev, Brezhnev, and Kosygin . . .❜ (H)

(*People's Daily*, Peking, 4 June 1967)

Why had China turned against Russia? China's view of Communism's future was very different from Russia's. Mao thought in terms of a world-wide struggle that would never end. He felt that Russia's leaders were only interested in spreading Communism when it made the Soviet Union stronger. Mao was certain that China was the true follower of Marx and Lenin. Khruschev thought that Mao's views were dangerous.

A second cause of dispute was Khruschev's idea of peaceful co-existence with America. To Mao, America was no more than a 'paper tiger' – strong in theory, but weak in practice, as the Korean War seemed to prove. Mao believed that Communism should take a 'hard line' against the West. He condemned Khruschev's 'soft' approach. Moreover, Khruschev maintained that only America and Russia were true world powers.

F Trade between Russia and China 1959–66

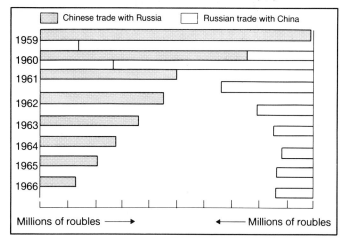

The split between Russia and China divided the whole Communist world. 65 out of 86 Communist parties took Russia's side. The Chinese were forced to rely even more on their own efforts and resources.

In 1969 Chinese troops killed 31 Russian guards in a dispute over where part of the 4500-mile frontier between the two countries should run. The crisis passed, but each side now feared the other. The Chinese feared Russia's nuclear strength and rushed to build nuclear shelters. The Russians feared China's vast army and aggressive leaders.

By 1970 China and Russia had destroyed the 'two against one' line-up. Now there was a 'triangle' of world power. In the following decade, both Russia and China would try to improve their relations with America.

?????????????????

1 a Copy out the graph below. Now use the information on pages 14–15 and 44–45 to plot the changes in Sino–Soviet relations between 1950 and 1970.

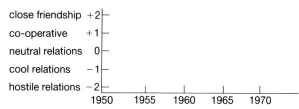

b Label your graph with the following events: Sino–Soviet Treaty; Russian views on Great Leap Forward; Khruschev's speech; Russia plans China's economy; Russia withdraws aid; border clashes; China explodes bomb; Korean war.
c Use your graph to write an account of relations between China and Russia, 1950–70.

26 Vietnam: a New Domino

Before the Second World War, Vietnam was part of the large French Empire in Indo-China. During the war, the country was occupied by the Japanese. Ho Chi Minh, a Communist, organised a guerilla force – the *Vietminh* – to drive out the Japanese. The Vietminh were backed by America. They were intent on creating an independent Vietnam, free from all foreign control.

Once the Japanese surrendered, Ho hoped the Vietminh would unite the whole country. But the French refused to give up their former Empire, and sent forces to reclaim Indo-China. The scene was set for a bitter guerilla war.

At first, America frowned upon French actions, but by 1949 the picture had changed. The Vietminh gained the support of Mao's Chinese Communists. Now, in American eyes, Indo-China had become yet another struggle against Communist expansion. So America supplied the French with military aid.

A   Vietnam 1954–60

1954
Geneva decisions:
1 Vietnam split into two
2 Dividing line 17°N
3 Free elections to reunite Vietnam by 1956
4 Cambodia, Laos: independent, neutral states
5 All foreign troops to be withdrawn

1954
Ho Chi Minh sets up Communist government in North. Confident of uniting Vietnam in elections

1954
Government of South Vietnam set up – led by President Diem

1954 →
Communist supporters in South trained in guerilla warfare by North Vietnamese

1954
America fears Communist success in elections. Supports South

1955
American advisers take over South Vietnam's armed forces. CIA step up operation against Vietcong in South

1956–7
America continues to support Diem – although his government corrupt, less democratic, more military

1958–9
Increased Vietcong guerilla activity in South

1959–60
South Vietnamese Government unpopular. Vietcong win peasant support in countryside. In towns VC mount bomb attacks against political enemies

Despite this, 8000 French troops were killed at Dien Bien Phu in 1954. It was a major defeat. France surrendered. The Great Powers met at Geneva in Switzerland to decide what to do. **A** shows the outcome of these talks, and the events which followed.

To America, Vietnam looked like another Asian 'domino'. America would have to help South Vietnam against the Communist North, or risk South East Asia falling under Communist control.

Meanwhile, Ho Chi Minh's Communist Government sent help and encouragement to the Communist guerilla force – the *Vietcong* – fighting in the South.

Massive amounts of American arms and money failed to stop the spread of Vietcong influence. In 1961 President Kennedy decided to send military advisors to South Vietnam. By 1962 there were 16 500 US troops in Vietnam, assisting South Vietnamese troops against the Vietcong. In 1964 the new American President, Lyndon Johnson, declared his determination not to 'lose Vietnam' to Communism:

❝I am not going to be the President who saw South East Asia go the way China went.❞ **(B)**

Johnson decided to *escalate* (greatly increase) the American presence in Vietnam **(C)**. Within 18 months, the USA was involved in a full-scale land and air war. The American air force pounded military targets and Vietcong supply routes. But they faced a determined enemy, as journalist James Cameron reported:

❝Every aspect of life is dominated by this mood of siege . . . air raid shelters, rifles stacked at the corners of paddy fields, great posters, aircraft recognition charts, weapon identifications 'roccet', 'bom' . . . When arms drills were signalled they were taken deadly seriously.❞ **(D)**

Even in 1968 Cameron doubted the success of the Americans' tactics:

❝There was a sense of outrage. By what right do these airmen intrude over a country with which they are not formally at war? Who gave these people the sanction to drop their bombs on roads, bridges, houses, to blow up the harvest, to destroy people of whom they know nothing? Would this sort of thing blow Communism out of their heads?❞ **(E)**

Despite the bombing, North Vietnam continued to supply the Vietcong in South Vietnam with ever-increasing amounts of aid. Much of it came from Russia:

❝At dusk the roads became alive. Engines were started and

C Number of US soldiers in Vietnam 1962–71

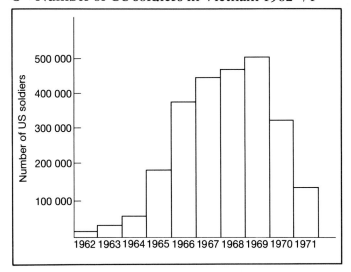

convoys emerged. There were miles of them – heavy, Russian-built lorries. By day North Vietnam is abandoned, by night it thuds and groans with movement. **(F)**

President Johnson hoped for a 'quick kill'. But the tactics of America's land forces in South Vietnam were based on several errors of judgement:

First, Americans were told to fight for 'the hearts and minds' of the Vietnamese. But how would the peasants react to events such as **G** (described by an American soldier who was involved):

Off to the right a woman's head appeared from some bushes. All the GIs started firing at her. The bullets riddled the woman's body. The men were oblivious to everything but slaughter. They just kept shooting at her. You could see the bones flying in the air, chip by chip. **(G)**

And what of the damage to the land itself? Richard Hamer, an American journalist, visited Vietnam in 1970:

To move about Vietnam today is to view the far side of the moon. This is now a land of bomb craters and shell holes, of deserted and ruined hamlets, of abandoned rice paddies. It is a country of refugees . . . once the rice bowl of Asia – now unable to feed itself. **(H)**

Second, America believed that it could 'win' the war in Vietnam. France had already tried and failed, but America could

simply not believe that the US could be defeated by a bunch of guerillas in black pyjamas. **(J)**

The reality of guerilla warfare was very different:

. . . this enemy is invisible . . . it is not just the people but the land itself – unfamiliar . . . frightening . . . it can be that field ahead littered with land mines . . . The enemy can

be the kind who comes out smiling and then lobs a grenade . . . or that bent old lady carrying a watermelon. **(K)**

You walk down a road between rice paddies. Vietnamese are in every paddy. Then, a mortar shell lands right in the middle of the patrol. A couple of guys are dead, others are screaming in agony with a leg or arm blown off, or their guts hanging out. Did one of them (the peasants) lob the mortar? If so which one? Should you kill all of them or none of them? **(L)**

Third, America's politicians thought that victory was worth any sacrifice. But there was a limit to the cost, and losses of men, that the American people would accept. By the late 1960s peace protestors outside the White House were chanting:

Hey, hey, LBJ! (President Johnson) *How many kids did you kill today?* **(M)**

By 1970 opposition to the American presence in Vietnam was widespread:

One does not use napalm (a chemical weapon which inflicts terrible burns) *on villages and hamlets sheltering civilians . . . if one is attempting to persuade these people of the rightness of one's cause. One does not blast hamlets to dust with high explosives from jet planes miles in the sky without warning – if one is attempting to woo the people living there to the goodness of one's cause . . . One does not defoliate* (destroy vegetation in) *a country and deform its people with chemicals if one is attempting to persuade them of the foe's evil nature.* **(N)**

In a decade of fighting in Vietnam, America would come to realise its errors of judgement – the hard way.

??????????????
1 What ideas emerged from the Geneva talks in 1954? How realistic were these ideas?

2 Explain what is meant by:
  a the Vietminh;
  b the Vietcong;
  c escalation;
  d guerilla warfare?

3 Imagine you are one of the following people. Describe how you feel about the fighting in Vietnam and the American involvement in the war.
  ● a North Vietnamese peasant (see **D, E, F**)
  ● a South Vietnamese peasant (see **G, H**)
  ● an American GI (see **G, J, L**)

4 How and why did America become involved in the Vietnam War? What problems did the Americans face in fighting the war? How successful were they?

27 Guerilla!

How would you have managed in the Vietnam War if you had been either an American GI or a Vietcong soldier? This game is for two players. You will need a die, two counters and a copy of the score chart below.

Players: one represents a Vietcong unit of 20 men; the other represents an American platoon of 50 men.

Aim: to gain control of a zone of South Vietnam, 100 km west of Saigon.

Objectives:

Vietcong unit	US platoon
To win the support of the South Vietnamese peasants	
To wage a guerilla war against the US forces	To find and destroy guerilla forces
To protect supply lines from North Vietnam	To cut Vietcong supply lines from the North
To recruit support among South Vietnamese peasants	To prevent the Vietcong gaining peasant support

Rules

1 Take it in turn to throw the die, and move forward the number of places it shows, starting from GO. Each 'round' of the board represents a three-month campaign.

2 If you land on a CHANCE square, read the 'action' for that square on your side's CHANCE chart. (There are enough 'chances' for two rounds). The numbers in the bottom right-hand corner of each box show whether the 'action' has been a success (+) or a failure (−). Fill in the score on the score chart, and keep a record of what happened to your side from the Chance chart.

3 The round finishes when a player crosses the GO line again. Both players must then add up their (+) and (−) scores, take the (−) from the (+) to find the total, and then read off the result on the Totals chart. For example, if you scored +35 points, this score falls between +25 and +50 − so the area of the zone under your side's control is 60 per cent.

4 At the end of each round, use your score chart and your record of the 'Chance' actions to judge your side's success or failure.

5 Keep on playing and checking your scores to see if the zone changes hands over a series of campaigns.

Key			
US	United States	**VC**	Vietcong
GI	General Infantry	**SV**	South Vietnamese
USAF	United States Airforce	**NV**	North Vietnamese

Score Chart

Team: ....

Round	Points (+)	(−)	Total points	% of zone under control
(Example)	20			
		10		
	5		+15	50

Totals Chart

Score per round	% of zone controlled
+125	100
+100	90
+ 75	80
+ 50	70
+ 25	60
0	50
− 25	40
− 50	30
− 75	20
−100	10
−125	0

?????????????????

After the group/form has played *Guerilla*:

1 Use your experience of the game to make brief notes on the war in Vietnam. Think about the following points.

Vietcong	United States
Tactics against the US	Tactics against the VC
Losses of personnel	Troop losses
Success in gaining peasant support and controlling villages	Success in making villages 'safe' and breaking VC supply lines
Difficulties in getting equipment	Superior fire power
The effect of the war on the South Vietnamese peasants	

2 Imagine you are a South Vietnamese peasant. What are your feelings about the war and how it was fought? What do you think of the US forces; the Vietcong?

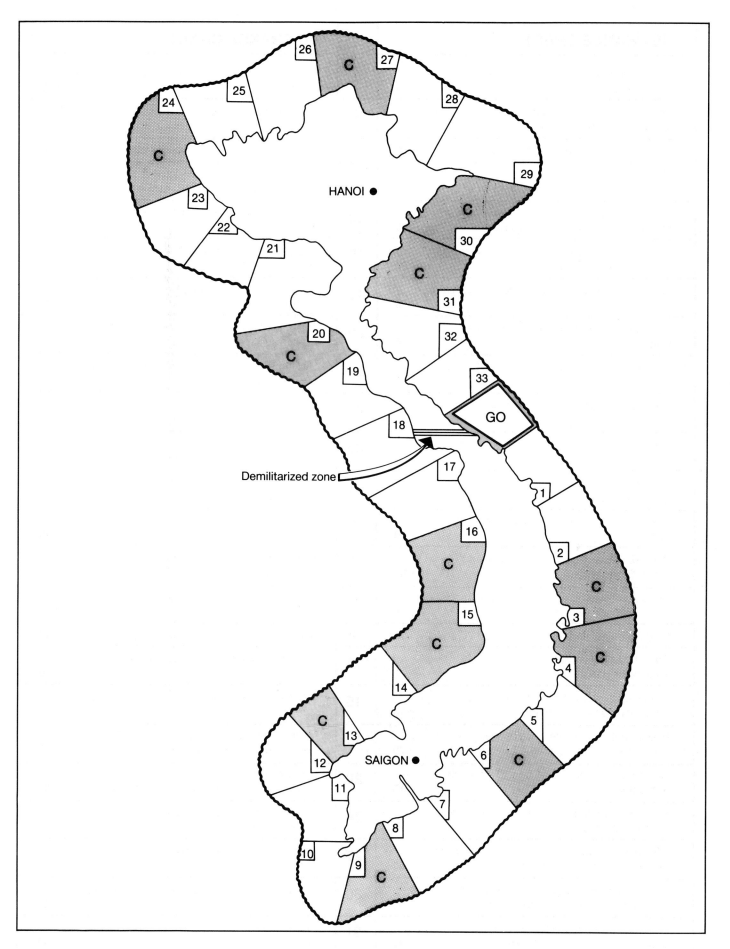

Demilitarized zone

HANOI ●

SAIGON ●

GO

US CHANCE CHART		VC CHANCE CHART

US CHANCE CHART		VC CHANCE CHART
Helicopter ferrying seven platoon members is destroyed by VC missile −10	3	Ambush American patrol crossing rice field and kill 15 GIs +70
No patrols while USAF drop napalm on cleared land between 'safe' villages +10	4	US destruction of villages restricts food supplies −20
Platoon member killed by booby trap −10	6	Unit receives supplies of Russian weapons +20
Platoon members push three VC prisoners out of helicopter +30	9	VC propaganda shows US forces as brutal and corrupt. One village joins VC cause +50
Platoon destroys village suspected of harbouring VC stores. Peasants flee +50	13	Unit member killed by land mine during a night march −5
Village hostile to US after cruelty by SV forces; may turn to VC for help −20	15	Village won over to VC by the promise of land ownership under Communism +50
Peasant village agrees to be resettled in a 'safe' area +50	16	NV infiltrators bring weapons down the Ho Chi Minh trail +20
Drug-taking among GIs increases. Morale worsens −5	20	Three unit members killed by US mine whilst moving supplies at night −15
Platoon captures an underground VC bunker with stores and weapons +30	24	Unit forced to shelter from carpet bombing raids by B52s. Four killed −15
Jeep destroyed by VC mine. Two GIs dead −10	27	Morale boosted by news of NV troops moving south with supplies +20
Platoon moved to defend Saigon due to threat of VC offensive +5	30	Unit destroys US helicopter with a land-launched missile +30
Platoon help clear wide road verges to deny the VC cover for ambushes +10	31	No operations because of heavy US bombing. No casualties −5
GI killed by VC booby trap whilst checking a bridge −10	3	Village made 'safe' by US troops is retaken by VC +50
Platoon makes village 'safe' – clears land around it and erects fence +50	4	USAF bombing of Ho Chi Minh Trail. Mines in short supply −20
News of anti-war demonstrations in USA reaches Vietnam. Morale worsens −5	6	Unit launches night attack on US supply dump. Kills six GIs +30
Patrol captures and shoots suspected VC agent +20	9	VC massacre 50 people in a US 'safe' village +10
Army investigates drug-taking and four GI addicts are transferred −5	13	Unit wins control of village by threats of torture +50
Morale boosted by 'no patrols' order whilst USAF bombs VC supply lines +10	15	Unit member killed whilst setting up a booby trap −5
Platoon patrols 'free fire' zone between two 'safe' villages. Shoots three VC suspects +20	16	VC intelligence reports US 'search and destroy' patrols nearby. Unit hides +5
No operations whilst USAF sprays the jungle with defoliants +15	20	Supplies not getting through because jungle tracks have been exposed by defoliants −30
Platoon attack large VC hideout. 10 VC killed, stores destroyed +70	24	Unit persuades fleeing villagers to stay put and hide VC guerillas +40
Village turns down US help because US cannot guarantee protection against VC −50	27	Two unit members killed by GI patrol whilst crossing 'free fire' zone −20
Platoon destroys village, 100 peasants shot because they are suspected of helping VC +50	30	Shortage of mortars because of US bombing of Cambodia −20
American TV team goes on patrol and films the death of a GI caused by VC mine −10	31	Unit attacks village loyal to the SV and destroys it +50

28 The Middle East 1

A The importance of the Suez Canal

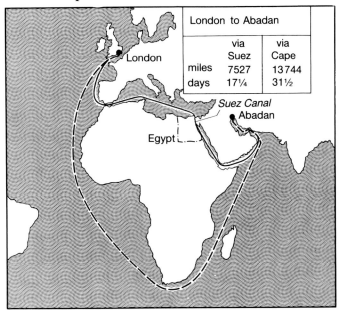

London to Abadan		
	via Suez	via Cape
miles	7527	13744
days	17¼	31½

By the 1950s Western Europe and America were relying more and more on oil supplies from the Middle East. Without oil, the West's economic and military power would collapse. The Suez Canal (see **A**) was a vital supply-route for the West.

The oil-producing countries of the Middle East were poor and backward. They needed to sell oil to modernise their countries.

Within the Middle East one issue dominated: the conflict over Israel. In 1948 Israel had been set up, with the West's backing, as a homeland for the Jews. It was formed from the former Arab lands of Palestine. Arab countries, such as Egypt and Syria, objected to Israel's existence. The issue had already caused one bitter war in 1948, between the Arabs and the Jews. The West feared that future Arab–Jew conflicts might upset world peace and threaten the vital oil supplies from the Middle East.

The Middle East was so important that it could not escape the Cold War. **B** shows that both America and Russia had reasons for being interested in the area. Since the early 1950s America had been taking steps to gain influence in, and support from, Middle East countries (**C**). By 1955 Russia's new leaders were ready to play an active role. America's Secretary of State warned that:

for the first time the Russians are making a determined effort to move into the Middle East, where two thirds of the world's known oil reserves are located. **(D)**

Great Power interest centred upon Egypt. Her new President, Gamal Nasser, was determined to strengthen Egypt by any means possible. Nasser's views interested Russia, since Egypt's earlier leaders had been pro-Western in outlook.

America became unsure of Nasser, who seemed intent on making Egypt the leader of the Arab world. For Egypt to become stronger, it needed to modernise. Nasser planned to build a huge dam across the River Nile at Aswan. It would provide electric power and irrigation for crops. Since building it would cost far more than Egypt could afford, Nasser sought a large

B Reasons for Great Power interest

Factor	Reason
Strategic Position	The Middle East is a land link to three large continents: Asia, Africa and Europe.
Foreign influence ★	The old great powers in the Middle East – Britain and France – are losing their influence. **America** should step in to prevent Russia doing so.
☽	**Russia** should make efforts to have more influence in the Middle East.
Israel/Palestine ★	**America** supports the new state of Israel and intends to give large amounts of aid, including military supplies.
☽	**Russia** supports Arab countries, like Egypt, which object to the seizing of Arab lands to set up Israel.
Containment/ encirclement ★	By forming alliances with Middle Eastern Countries **America** could complete the 'containment' of Communism.
☽	Gaining the friendship of Middle Eastern countries would break America's encirclement of the USSR.
Oil (economic) ★	**American** oil supplies from the Persian Gulf (through Suez) must be protected.
☽	Since the USA and its allies are so dependent on Middle Eastern oil, the Middle East is a weak spot for the West.
Oil (political and military) ★	Any Russian influence in the Middle East is a threat to the West.
☽	In future East–West conflict, **Russia** could disrupt the Middle East oil supplies to the West.

C US influence in the Middle East, 1951–55

1951	British Iran Oil Co *nationalised* (taken over) by Iranian Government.
1953	Iran threatens to sell-out to Russia.
1953	America secretly supplies the Shah (King) of Iran with military aid to overthrow the Government.
1954	Iran signs agreement to supply America and Western Europe with oil.
1955	**Baghdad Pact** – for defence and security in the Middle East. America got Britain, Iran, Turkey, Pakistan and Iraq to sign. This was the final move in America's policy of *Containment*. The Soviet Union was now surrounded by hostile countries and American bases.
1959	**CENTO** Iraq left the pact. America joined, to form the Central Treaty Organisation.

loan from overseas. Khruschev told Nasser that Russia would provide the loan. America, worried about Russian influence in Egypt, outbid the Russian offer. Complicated talks followed. In the end Egypt accepted a large loan from America and Britain.

Then, without warning, America withdrew its offer on the grounds that Egypt could not afford the interest payments. Nasser was stung by this public insult. In a speech in Alexandria on 26 July he put forward his plan. Egypt would *nationalise* (take over) the Suez Canal, which was owned by a British/French company.

❝*We shall build the High Dam . . . industrialise Egypt and compete with the West – with the revenue from the Canal we shall not look to Britain or the USA for their grant.*❞ (E)

The revenue from the canal came from tolls or taxes on shipping, and amounted to about 30 million pounds a year.

Britain and France were furious. Anthony Eden, Britain's Prime Minister, said

❝*a man with Colonel Nasser's record cannot be allowed to have his thumb on our windpipe.*❞ (F)

Britain, France and Israel began to make secret plans to retake the Canal zone of Egypt.

America, which had supplied Egypt with arms in the past, decided to test Nasser's loyalties. Nasser's request for American weapons was refused. Nasser turned to the Warsaw Pact countries.

❝*Czechoslovakia is to supply arms in exchange for Egyptian cotton and rice.*❞ (G)　　　(The Times, 27 September 1956)

America wondered if Nasser would develop further Communist links.

America's greatest shock came from its NATO allies. Without informing America, first Israel and then Britain and France moved against Egypt. Their plan, agreed on 14 October, was:

❝*that Israel should be invited* (by Britain and France) *to attack Egypt across the Sinai dessert, and that Britain and France should then order both sides to withdraw their forces* (from the Suez Canal zone), *in order to permit an Anglo–French force to intervene and occupy the Canal, on the pretext of saving it from damage by fighting.*❞ (H)

Egypt refused to 'withdraw' from her own territory. So Britain bombed Egypt on 31 October, and on 5 November dropped paratroops to drive the Egyptians away from the Canal. J shows Nasser's reaction: he closed the Suez Canal. The West's economic lifeline was, for a time, cut.

The British and French action stung the Great Powers into movement. Russia, seeing a chance to gain

J A blockade of old ships closed off the Suez Canal in November 1956. It was re-opened almost two years later

L   American and Russian involvement in the Middle East by 1967

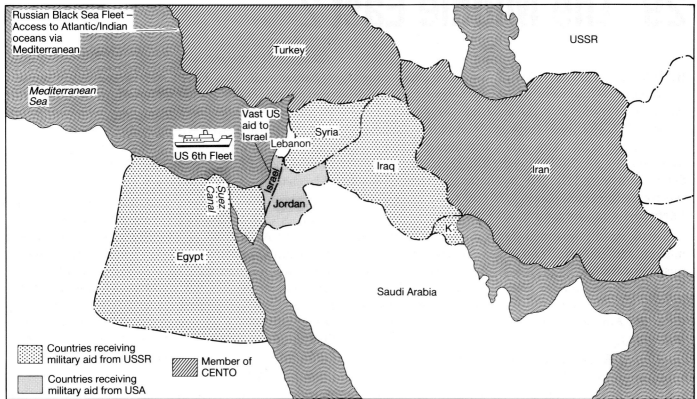

Countries receiving military aid from USSR

Countries receiving military aid from USA

Member of CENTO

Egypt's friendship, issued a threat to Britain:

' The British Government must put an end to the war in Egypt. We are determined to crush the aggressor and restore peace to the Middle East. There are countries now which need not send army or air force . . . but could use other means, such as rocket techniques. ' (**K**)

America threatened not to supply Britain with oil from South America (its only source now Suez was blocked) if British forces were not withdrawn from Suez. The UN ordered Britain and France to withdraw, and they were forced to back down. European influence in the Middle East was over. America and Russia began to jockey for position in an already unstable area!

Russia's support for Egypt drew the two countries closer together. By standing up to Britain and France, Nasser had shown himself to be the leader of the Arab world. The Aswan Dam, the cause of 'the Suez affair' was financed by Russia. Within two years the Canal re-opened, under UN control.

America tried to strengthen its friendship with the oil-producing states. In March 1957 America announced the 'Eisenhower Doctrine'. Military and economic aid from America was promised to all who wanted it as a defence against Communism. The Lebanon and Jordan accepted, but Syria sided with the Soviet Union. The following year American troops were

forced into action to defend the Lebanon against a Syrian-backed revolution.

The Middle East states wanted no part in the Cold War, and voted so, unanimously, at the UN in 1959. Direct American and Russian involvement lessened, only to be replaced by a long-running Arab–Israeli conflict. By now, however, as **L** shows, the two Great Powers had chosen which sides they would back.

??????????????

1 Why was the Suez Canal so important to the West (**A**)?

2 a Why did both America and Russia have interests in the Middle East (see **B**)?
b How successful was America in securing her Middle Eastern interests (see **B** and **C**)?

3 a Why might statements **E** and **G** worry America?
b What threat did Russia make to Britain to withdraw forces from Suez (**K**)?
c What threat did America make to Britain?

4 How did America and Russia try to gain friends in the Middle East after 1956? With what success?

29 The Middle East 2

By 1967 the Arab states, with Russia's help, had gained in strength. They were ready, once again, to attack Israel. To counter this threat, Israel struck first. On 5 June 1967, Israeli jets (supplied by America) destroyed ten Egyptian airfields in just a few hours. Egypt lost over 300 Russian-built aircraft. Later, the airforces of Syria, Jordan and Iraq were shattered. Having won control of the skies, Israel sent tanks and troops into Egypt, Syria and Jordan.

Russia rapidly re-armed Egypt and Syria with more modern and powerful tanks, aircraft and anti-aircraft missiles. Meanwhile, America supplied Israel with its latest weapons. America was in a difficult position. On the one hand it supported Israel against the Arabs; on the other, America depended on Arab oil supplies!

6 October 1973. An Arab attack took Israel by surprise. Most Israelis were preparing for Yom Kippur – a religious festival. At first, Egyptian and Syrian ground attacks were successful. Egypt's Russian-built missiles shot down many Israeli aircraft.

America acted quickly in making good Israel's losses. The Russians sent more supplies to the Arabs. Israeli forces held the Arab advance and then counter-attacked.

❛Israel claimed tonight that its outnumbered forces had succeeded in holding the Syrian attack in the Golan Heights and the attempt by Egypt to cross the Sinai.❜ **(A)**

(The Times, 8 October 1973)

B   Results of the Yom Kippur War 1973

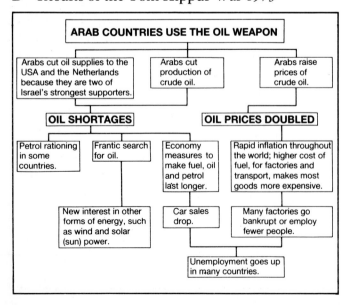

America, Russia, Egypt and Israel tried to set up a ceasefire to end the war. The Israelis rejected such attempts. With another Arab defeat looming, the Americans feared that Russia might send in troops. In response, President Nixon put American forces on a world-wide nuclear alert. The Middle East war threatened to escalate into a Third World War.

With Egypt and Syria looking beaten other Arab countries (the oil-producers) stepped in with a threat. The eight Arab members of OPEC (the Organisation of Petroleum Exporting Countries) said that America must stop arms supplies to Israel, or OPEC would impose cut-backs in oil supplies to America from the Middle East. Since America used oil for nearly half its energy needs, this was a serious threat. **B** shows the effects OPEC's action had on the West. By December 1973, OPEC had not only cut supplies but had increased the price of oil by four times!

Now, both Great Powers had good reasons to help end the war. Russia feared an Arab defeat. America was plunged by OPEC into an energy crisis. In the peace talks, America's need for oil outweighed her support for Israel. The result was a favourable settlement for Egypt.

The energy crisis of 1973–4 and the new-found power of OPEC made America and the West realise that they must be friendly with Arab countries. Since 1977 Egypt has looked more to America for aid than to Russia. America has been careful to gain the friendship of Saudi Arabia, the West's main supplier of oil, and OPEC's most powerful member.

After four wars between Arab and Jew in 25 years, America decided that the best way to safeguard Middle East oil supplies was to end the hostility between Egypt and Israel for good. If America could persuade Egypt to sign an agreement with Israel, then it could split Egypt from other Arab countries. This would make Israel safer, by dividing the Arab opposition. It would also swing Egypt away from Russia, because of her probable isolation amongst Arab nations.

The American efforts resulted in a Middle East Peace Treaty, signed at Camp David (USA) in 1979. President Carter's efforts were hailed as a triumph in the West.

❛The Foreign Ministers of Western Europe "hope that the outcome will be a further major step to a just, comprehensive and lasting peace".❜ **(C)**   (The Times, 19 September 1979)

As America hoped, Russia, now out of favour with

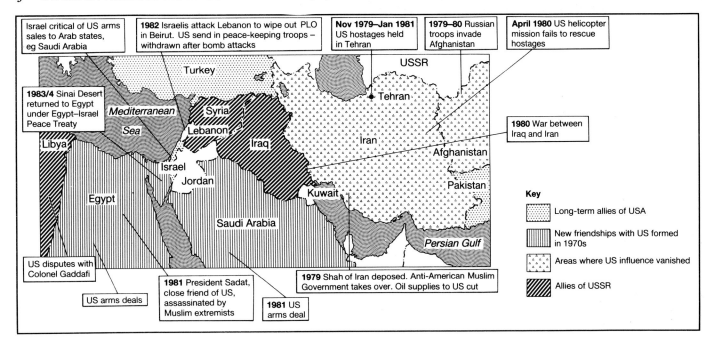

Israel critical of US arms sales to Arab states, eg Saudi Arabia

1982 Israelis attack Lebanon to wipe out PLO in Beirut. US send in peace-keeping troops – withdrawn after bomb attacks

Nov 1979–Jan 1981 US hostages held in Tehran

1979–80 Russian troops invade Afghanistan

April 1980 US helicopter mission fails to rescue hostages

1983/4 Sinai Desert returned to Egypt under Egypt–Israel Peace Treaty

1980 War between Iraq and Iran

US disputes with Colonel Gaddafi

US arms deals

1981 President Sadat, close friend of US, assassinated by Muslim extremists

1981 US arms deal

1979 Shah of Iran deposed. Anti-American Muslim Government takes over. Oil supplies to US cut

Key

Long-term allies of USA

New friendships with US formed in 1970s

Areas where US influence vanished

Allies of USSR

Egypt, believed that a separate treaty would make a full settlement to all the Middle East's problems more difficult to find:

The Camp David agreement is a betrayal of the Arab cause . . . and a complete surrender before the Israelis. **(D)**

(*Tass*, 20 September 1979)

At this point, the unstable nature of the Middle East produced a new factor: in Iran. Over many years America had developed close links with oil-rich Iran. Iran's leader, the Shah, had been helped into power by America. In return, the Shah had adopted pro-Western policies. In 1978 and 1979 a wave of strikes and demonstrations against the Shah swept through Iran. Many were organised by Iran's large Muslim population. They demanded a political revolution, based on the principles of *Islam* (the Muslim faith).

In October 1979 the Shah was forced to leave Iran. He went to America for medical treatment. Iran's new Muslim leader, the Ayatollah Khomeini, made his feelings clear:

In the name of God, death to your plots America. The USA is the main enemy of mankind. **(E)**

On 5 November 1979 headlines in *The Times* announced:

Mob Storms US Embassy. Send Us the Shah Call by Khomeini Students

400 students seized the American Embassy in Tehran yesterday and seized up to 100 hostages. The students said they would not realease the hostages until the deposed Shah is sent

back to Iran from his hospital bed in New York . . . Cheers turned to shouts of frenzy when two American flags were burned. **(F)**

The American hostages remained captive for 14 months. All attempts to gain their release failed. President Carter became desperate:

Failure of Iran Rescue . . . Eight Americans die . . . aircraft lost . . . A commando mission designed to rescue the hostages ended in failure and tragedy today. Eight American servicemen were killed . . . when a helicopter crashed into a transport plane on the ground in a remote desert area of Iran. **(G)**

Eventually, on 20 January 1981, the hostages were released (the Shah had by this time died). By now Iran and Iraq were at war. **H** shows the changes in American interest within the Middle East since 1973.

??????????????

1 Why did the Yom Kippur War seem, briefly, a threat to world peace?

2 How did America try to bring about an end to Egypt–Israel conflict after 1973? Why?

3 Use **H** to list the problems that America has had to face in the Middle East since 1979.

30 Detente 1

Russia, China and America had all learnt hard lessons about the limit of their powers. Each had suffered major setbacks – Russia over Cuba, America over Vietnam, and China over Russia. East and West were fully aware of the dangers, and cost, of the nuclear arms race. Was the time right for a change in relations between East and West?

As a new year dawned, in 1969, *The Times* thought so:

❝ 1 January 1969 *The Soviet Union is now showing every sign of wishing for some form of understanding with the United States.* ❞ (A)

The first step forward was in Europe. The West German leader, Willy Brandt, wanted to improve

E The badge worn by the American crew who took part in the Apollo–Soyuz space link-up

relations with Eastern Europe, especially East Germany. His *Ostpolitik* (Eastern Policy) achieved great success between 1966 and 1973. Agreements on frontiers and treaties were signed between West Germany and Warsaw Pact nations.

❝ Moscow, August 1970 *A good step . . . Herr Brandt arrived to sign the new treaty between his country and Russia against the use of force. It is a step forward. It makes a whole series of further steps possible.* ❞ (B)

In 1972, agreements between West and East Germany were signed in the Basic Treaty. More trade, cultural, sporting and personal contacts were to follow. None of this could have been possible without Russia's co-operation.

The ten years from 1969 to 1979 became the decade of *detente* (a French word meaning 'a relaxation of tension' between states). During these years America and Russia made efforts to reduce the areas of tension between them. At the same time, China and America worked hard to create a measure of friendship to replace their 20 years of hostility. Each Great Power had very different reasons for wanting detente as **C** shows.

Though detente saw East–West tension ease, relations between China and Russia stayed poor. Their quarrel left each Communist giant isolated, and this helped the cause of detente. Both China and Russia wished to be on good terms with America, for fear of what their Communist neighbour might do.

C Great Power motives for detente

America
- To drive a wedge between Russia and China.
- This would be to America's advantage in the fight against Communism in Vietnam (because Russia and China co-operated in supplying North Vietnam with arms).
- America's leaders – President Nixon and Secretary of State, Henry Kissinger – were keen to set up realistic working relations with Moscow and Peking.

Russia
- President Brezhnev was keen to extend Khruschev's idea of 'peaceful co-existence'.
- Brezhnev saw detente as a way to increase Russia's trade with the West and so develop Russia's economy in order to improve living standards within Russia.
- To decrease defence spending.
- To persuade the West to accept the post-war situation in Eastern Europe.
- To avoid Russia being the odd one out in the '2 against 1' line up: America, Russia, China. Russia was keen to create better relations with America.

China
- Her motives were forced upon her by the actions of the other two Great Powers.
- America had been hostile to China – her policy in South East Asia first over Korea, then Vietnam – worried China.
- Ever since the 1960 split with Russia, China feared Russia. China looked to America for friendship, to isolate Russia.
- China's leaders wanted to modernise the country – especially in farming, industry, science, technology and defence. Increased trade with the West would help to modernise China more quickly.

Detente between America and Russia took many forms – political, cultural, sporting, economic and scientific. **D** is an example of political detente. On 23 March 1972 *The Times* reported from Moscow:

'*Stars and Stripes Flies Over the Kremlin. Mr Nixon began his visit to the Soviet Union today, becoming the first American President to visit Moscow.* ' **(D)**

E shows an example of scientific detente. On 17 July 1975, three American astronauts met up with two Russian cosmonauts in space. Premier Brezhnev described this Apollo/Soyuz link up:

'*the flight was of historic significance . . . as a symbol of the present process of easing the international tension and the improvement of US–Soviet relations on the basis of peaceful co-existence. (It was) . . . a practical contribution between the USA and USSR in the interests of the peoples of both countries and in the interests of world peace.* ' **(F)**

In this spirit of detente, both sides made great efforts to achieve progress in the difficult area of arms control (see pages 58–59).

The high point of USA–USSR detente was the Helsinki Agreement of 1975. At Helsinki, in Finland, 35 states, including America and Russia, agreed that the frontiers of post-1945 Europe should be permanent. This pleased Russia. The Russians thought it meant that the West accepted the iron curtain as a fact of life and that Russia's influence in Eastern Europe could not be questioned. It was also agreed, at the demand of America's President Carter, that all states should respect 'human rights' such as freedom of thought and religion. By this, the West hoped that people in Communist

K Chairman Mao welcomes US President Nixon to China in 1972

countries would be given more freedom to express their views, without fear of arrest or imprisonment.

American–Russian detente was not so surprising. After all, both 'superpowers' had been through painful Cold War experiences. But how did detente develop between America and China? **G** shows members of the Chinese and American table-tennis teams, who played each other in Peking in 1971. The first sign of friendship in 20 years! A year later a return match was played in America. The sporting contest was matched, behind the scenes, with contact between government officials. 'Ping-pong diplomacy' was the first step in a new phase of relations. Tension gradually eased. But sticking points remain to detente.

One is America's support of Taiwan. For 20 years America backed Taiwan's claim to represent China at the United Nations.

There is drama on 25 October 1971 at the United Nations Headquarters in New York. Newspaper headlines reveal that:

'*China admitted to the UN. Taiwan expelled . . . UN delegates screamed, sang, shouted, pounded desks and even danced in the aisles.* ' **(H)**

The Times voices the widely held view that:

'*a wrong done to the world's largest country has at last been righted.* ' **(J)**

Later, in October 1971, the delegate from Communist China takes the China seat at the UN. America's

G Members of the US and Chinese table-tennis teams comparing technique

willingness to create detente is behind this change (although America hoped that 'both' Chinas could have seats at the UN).

American/Chinese relations warm. The American Secretary of State, Henry Kissinger, lays the foundation for a meeting of the countries' two leaders (**K**). President Nixon thinks that

❛*the chances of building a lasting peace* (between America and China) *are the best this century.*❜ (**L**)

Trade and travel agreements follow. Chinese leaders visit America in 1979. By 1979, America is ready to recognise Communist China as the legal government of China. Over 60 large American firms are set up in China. The amount of trade between America and China is likely to double between 1980 and 1985.

???????????????

1 a Copy the timechart below, and fill it in:

A Decade of Detente

Year		Main Events	
	Between East/ West in Europe	Between USA/USSR	Between USA/China
1969 1970 …			

2 Explain why, and how, the years 1969–79 developed into the decade of detente. (Use your timechart to help you.)

Your essay will need an *introduction* where you briefly set the scene; a *development* where you explain the 'how' and 'why'; and a brief *conclusion*. Here you should write your opinion of detente. First, organise these jumbled-up headings into a good order (1–5) for an essay.

Detente between China and America

Why each Great Power wanted detente

The practical results of detente

Detente between America and Russia

East–West detente in Europe

Can you use 1 and 5 as the basis for an introduction and conclusion? Re-read *Detente 1*. Then write the essay in your own words.

31 Detente 2

A The nuclear balance shifts

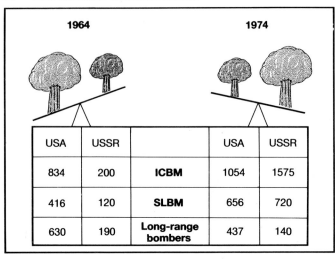

	1964			1974	
USA	USSR		USA	USSR
834	200	**ICBM**	1054	1575
416	120	**SLBM**	656	720
630	190	**Long-range bombers**	437	140

Getting America and Russia to agree on any military matters would be difficult. But both superpowers had strong motives for trying to achieve agreement. Limited co-operation in military affairs had begun after the 1962 Cuban Missile Crisis. Throughout the rest of the 1960s a variety of agreements were signed. Some were just between America and Russia, others involved many nations. Most had loopholes and weaknesses.

America and Russia continued the nuclear arms race (see **A**). But America was falling behind. In conventional armed strength, the Soviet-controlled Warsaw Pact forces in Europe outnumbered the NATO forces (**B**). For both Great Powers the cost of the arms race was collosal.

B NATO and Warsaw Pact forces: a comparison

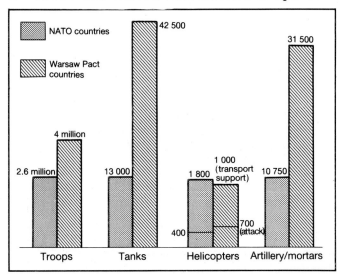

C Limits agreed at SALT 1

Weapons Allowed	USA	USSR
Long-range missiles (ICBMs)	1000	1600
Long-range multi-target warheads	10 000	4000
Submarine-launched missiles (SLBMs)	650	700
Multi-target submarine-launched warheads	6000	2000
Medium-range missiles	1600	
Heavy bombers	500	

N.B. Russia has fewer nuclear warheads than America, but has bigger bombs.

In the climate of political detente, could the Great Powers come to some agreement about reducing or limiting nuclear arms? In 1969 America and Russia began SALT talks (Strategic Arms Limitation Talks). The aim was to slow down the arms race by limiting the stock of long-range nuclear weapons. Covered in the talks were ICBMs (Inter-Continental Ballistic Missiles – long-range missiles), SLBMs (Submarine Launched Ballistic Missiles), and ABMs (Anti-Ballistic Missile defences). The number of land and submarine missiles and aircraft able to deliver nuclear warheads was frozen. C shows the agreed limits.

The USSR was allowed to have more missiles, in total, than America. This was because many American missiles were capable of carrying several warheads, each aimed at separate targets. Each side was only allowed to have 100 ABMs on each of two sites. This cut down defence costs for both countries, since a complete shield of ABMs was almost impossible and very expensive. Each side was allowed to use spy satellites to check that the other was not breaking the arms limits.

Both countries seemed pleased with SALT. D gives the Soviet view:

SALT talks show that despite differences an improvement in relations between the USSR and USA is quite possible. The agreements signed must check the arms drive, which creates the

F A British newspaper cartoon from 1976. It shows Henry Kissinger, US Secretary of State (on the left) with Leonid Brezhnev, the Soviet leader

...the exchange of sweet nothings.

...covering up his treaty violations.

...knowing when to give something for nothing.

G Limits agreed at SALT 2

Weapons Allowed	USA	USSR
Long-range missiles (ICBMs)	1054	1398
Long-range multi-target missiles	550	608
Submarine-launched missiles (SLBMs)	656	950
Multi-target submarine-launched missiles	496	144
Heavy bombers	573	156

threat of nuclear conflict, and diverts vast means from creative objectives. (D)

President Nixon, for America, said that:

a declaration of this magnitude (importance) could only have been taken by two countries which had chosen to place their relations on a new foundation of restraint, co-operation, and confidence. (E)

F is a British cartoon, commenting on the agreement.

The SALT 1 agreement was only for five years. So further talks began, called SALT 2, first with President Nixon, then Ford and then Carter. The new talks were very complicated. America and Russia were trying to agree on arms limits involving new weapons not covered by SALT 1. G gives details of the agreement reached in 1979. President Carter thought SALT 2 was

the most detailed, far-reaching, comprehensive treaty in the history of arms control. (H)

SALT 2 was due to last until 1985, but an event on Christmas Day 1979 was to destroy not only SALT 2 but the whole process of detente . . .

??????????????

1 a Study **A**. What, in 1974, would these figures tell America's leaders?
b What does SALT mean?
c What was the aim of SALT?

2 a Do you think the SALT 1 agreement was fair to both sides?
b Is the Russian view of SALT 1 (**D**) in agreement with the American view (**E**)?

3 a Why were SALT 2 talks more complicated than SALT 1 ones?
b Use **G** to draw a graph showing the SALT 2 agreements.

4 What do you think the cartoonist who drew **F** thought of detente? How useful are cartoons as historical evidence?

32 Afghanistan

Christmas Day, 1979. Television news reports that Russian troops have invaded Afghanistan. First details of the events are hazy. An eye-witness at Kabul (the Afghanistan capital) airport 'saw between 150 and 200 Russian soldiers armed with rifles walk past . . .'

As news filtered out, events became clearer:

Large Russian Force in Afghanistan . . . The Soviet Union made a massive airlift into Kabul over Christmas on December 25/26 and now have concentrated five divisions along the border. **(A)** (The Times, 27 December 1979)

Between 24–27 December 350 aircraft landed Russian troops at Kabul. On 28 December Kabul Radio announced that the Afghan President Hafizullah Amin had been executed after being tried and found guilty of 'crimes against the state'. In his place a new President, Barbek Karmel, was chosen. He announced:

we will remain a faithful member of the UN and the non-aligned countries. **(B)**

Could this be possible? Afghanistan had been a founder member of the non-aligned states of Africa and Asia, ever since 1955. But since then her leaders had looked to the Communist world, and had sided with the Soviet Union. Now, Afghanistan seemed firmly in the grip of Russia. C suggests why Russia was so interested in Afghanistan.

Between 29 and 31 December Russian ground forces crossed into Afghanistan. By 1 January 1980, 50 000 troops were judged to be in the country. President Brezhnev gave the official Soviet version of events:

Russia says Military Airlift was Justified . . . President Brezhnev today offered his 'warmest congratulations to the new leaders of Afghanistan'. **(D)** (The Times, 28 December 1979)

C   Reasons for Russian interest in Afghanistan

- Control of Afghanistan would put pressure on the Middle East – the oil lifeline to the USA and Western Europe could be threatened.
- The political scene in Afghanistan was unstable, and had got worse since spring 1979.
- Russian control of Afghanistan would counter American and Chinese influence in the area (both gave aid to neighbouring Pakistan).
- The Muslim Revolution in neighbouring Iran, in 1979, might spread across to Afghanistan. A Russian take-over would remove this threat. It would also settle Russia's own Muslim population (30 million) at the same time.

He justified the airlift of troops by saying that

they had responded to an urgent request from the Kabul Government for help. **(E)**

The same day, over the Moscow–Washington hotline, Brezhnev told President Carter of America that he

had been invited in by the Afghan Government to come in and protect it from some outside, third nation, threat . . . (Russia would) *remove forces from Afghanistan as soon as the situation stabilized.* **(F)**

On 28 December the USA sent a formal note of protest to Russia. The next day, President Carter described Russia's presence in Afghanistan as 'gross interference . . . a threat to peace'. He went on

in the next few days the leaders of the world must make it clear to the Soviets that they cannot violate (upset) *world peace . . . without paying severe consequences.* **(G)**

China's reaction left no doubt as to their feelings. Her leaders, according to a newspaper report:

Liken Afghan Coup to the Rape of Prague . . . China said today that the Soviet Union's first large-scale military intervention in a Third World country meant it could no longer pose as an angel of World Peace. **(H)**

The *Peking People's Daily* of 1 January 1980 saw Russia's actions as a:

stepping stone for a southward thrust towards Pakistan and the (Indian) *sub-continent. There will be no peace in Southern Asia with Soviet soldiers in strategic Afghanistan.* **(J)**

China protested to the UN about Russia's action and offered support to the Afghan guerilla fighters – the *Mujahidin* – who had started guerilla warfare against the Russians. China also promised military support to Pakistan.

K shows why America and China were so interested in this area. L shows the actions America took in 1980.

On 5 January the Russian news agency, *Tass*, described the American actions as a 'flagrant violation of detente'. On 12 January *Pravda*, the official Russian newspaper, reported that President Brezhnev 'blamed the USA for the worsening world situation'. He spoke of the

mountain of lies built up around the events. A shameless anti-Soviet campaign is being mounted. (The USA is) *an absolutely unreliable partner, whose leadership is capable – at any moment – of cancelling treaties and agreements.* **(M)**

K American and Chinese interests in Afghanistan

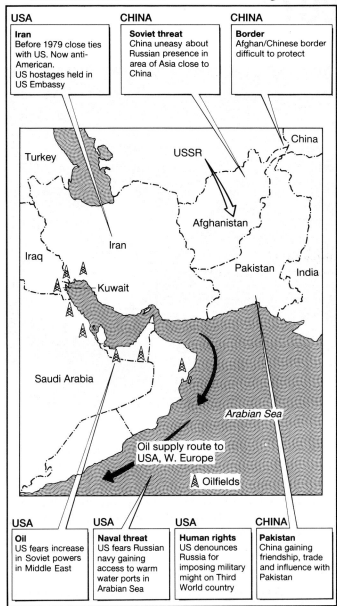

USA
Iran
Before 1979 close ties with US. Now anti-American.
US hostages held in US Embassy

CHINA
Soviet threat
China uneasy about Russian presence in area of Asia close to China

CHINA
Border
Afghan/Chinese border difficult to protect

Oil supply route to USA, W. Europe

Oilfields

USA
Oil
US fears increase in Soviet powers in Middle East

USA
Naval threat
US fears Russian navy gaining access to warm water ports in Arabian Sea

USA
Human rights
US denounces Russia for imposing military might on Third World country

CHINA
Pakistan
China gaining friendship, trade and influence with Pakistan

In late January President Carter withdrew America from the Moscow Olympics. He described Russia as an 'unsuitable site for a festival meant to celebrate peace and goodwill'.

Whatever the cause of Russia's action in Afghanistan, the result was the total collapse of detente. As the new decade dawned, America and Russia seemed on the verge of a new Cold War.

Five years on Russian troops remain in Afghanistan. The Mujahidin guerrillas, though poorly equipped, have control of much of the countryside. Russian troops have a difficult time keeping land supply routes safe from guerilla attacks:

❝*Mujahidin Kill Soviet General . . . The big Russian offensive begun two weeks ago has had its first important*

L Action taken by America in 1980

Arms talks/SALT 2: President Carter advised the US Senate not to *ratify* (agree to) the arrangements for nuclear arms limits already agreed between America and Russia.

Military task force: A US Navy Task Force of 1800 marines was sent to the Arabian Sea to protect oil routes.

Economic sanctions: President Carter told Russia that America would: *'halt or reduce exports to the Soviet Union'.* In particular, *'17 million tons of grain (previously agreed) will not be delivered'.* Also, a *'suspension of sale of high technology goods – including computers and oil drilling equipment'.* Finally, a *'severe loss of Soviet fishing privileges in US waters'.*

Olympic boycott: *'In order to make the world realise how serious a threat the Soviet invasion of Afghanistan is'* . . . President Carter threatened to withdraw from the 1980 Olympic Games due to take place in Moscow.

Military aid: America agreed to increase aid to Pakistan and told Russia and Pakistan that the USA would support Pakistan using 'armed force if necessary'.

Aid to Afghan rebels: America agreed to support the Afghan guerillas in their fight against Russian forces.

casualty – a general. He died when his helicopter was shot down on October 9 by resistance marksmen near Herat. ❞ **(N)**

(*The Times*, 26 October 1983)

America and China have had to accept that Afghanistan has become the first Russian satellite in Southern Asia. Neither country has done much to support the Afghan rebels. But their fears of further Russian expansion in the area have so far been unfounded.

??????????????

1 a Why do you think that the first Russian troops were airlifted into Afghanistan (**A**)?
b How realistic do Russia's reasons for invasion seem to you (**E**, **F**)?
c How did the other Great Powers react to Russia's action (**G**, **H**)?

2 a Which of America's actions in **L** do you think would be: the most effective; the least effective?
b How would an American boycott of the Moscow Olympics affect Russia?

3 a Why did Russia blame America for threatening the process of detente?
b Was there any future for detente, after Afghanistan?

4 Why do you think the Russian troops have so far failed to wipe out the Afghan rebels? What do you think will be the future of Afghanistan?

33 A New Arms Race?

With the end of detente, the two Superpowers entered into another round of the arms race. Despite detente, world military spending rose throughout the 1970s. Three quarters of that total was spent by NATO and Warsaw Pact forces.

In 1980 Ronald Reagan became President of the USA. He, like many other Americans, was concerned about nuclear arms. Russia seemed to be expanding her military power faster than America (**A**). Reagan decided to increase America's defence spending, raising it from 178 billion dollars in 1981 to 367 billion in 1986.

America and her NATO allies were also concerned about the development of new Russian weapons, not included in any arms limitation talks. According to NATO:

❝ *The Soviet Union, experience shows, is willing to threaten or use force beyond its own frontiers – Afghanistan . . . shows this clearly. The Soviet Union is devoting . . . a large part of its resources to a massive military build-up, far exceeding its defence needs.* ❞ (**B**)

To counter this threat, America pressed ahead with the introduction of new weapons of its own, such as **C**.

Many people in Western Europe feared the Russian threat. By December 1979 there were over 600 Russian SS-20 missiles in position. In 1979 NATO agreed that a total of 464 American *Cruise missiles* should be *deployed* (sited) in Western Europe, **D**.

C   The US *Cruise* missile

In some countries the arrival of Cruise missiles has been met by demonstrations by peace groups. In Britain, Cruise missile sites such as Greenham Common have been the scene of women's peace protests (**E**). Elsewhere, groups such as CND (Campaign for Nuclear Disarmament) have protested about the Great Powers' reliance on nuclear weapons as the best way to preserve peace.

The NATO decision to deploy Cruise missiles worsened East–West relations. In 1981 President Reagan an-

A   The arms race since 1976

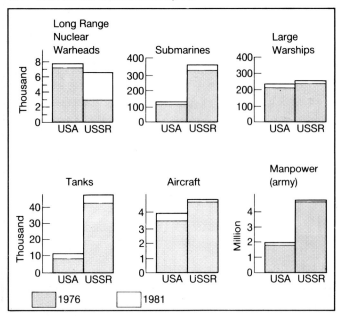

D   Cruise missiles in Western Europe

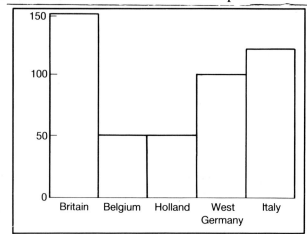

nounced that America had developed a new type of bomb – the *neutron* bomb. This has the effect of killing many people, without destroying much property. The Russians feared that such weapons showed that America's leaders believed they could win a limited nuclear war in Europe.

This was a new idea. Before this, both sides believed that a 'balance of terror' existed in the arms race. This balance was based on the idea of MAD (Mutually Assured Destruction) – that is, since each side has the ability to destroy the other many times over, neither side dare attack for fear of certain destruction.

The fear of sudden attack by Russia led America to consider very expensive defence systems. In 1982 President Reagan decided that America would install the MX missile. This is a powerful missile with many warheads, placed on underground tracks, which could be launched from different underground silos. 100 MX missiles will be in place by 1986.

The worsening relations between America and Russia also showed in arms talks. New talks began in Geneva, Switzerland, in 1981, but not before President Reagan had threatened Russia with the alternative:

❛an Arms Race they cannot win❜ (F)

Reagan proposed START talks (Strategic Arms Reduction Talks), based on a reduction of nuclear forces, rather than the unsuccessful talks on limitation. One example was his so-called 'zero-option', by which America proposed to scrap its plans to install Cruise missiles in Europe, in return for Russia's agreement to dismantle her SS-20 missiles, already in place. Russia rejected the 'zero-option'. In 1985, under the direction of the new Russian Premier, Yuri Andropov, Russia walked out of the Geneva arms talks.

Increasingly, the arms race has been extended into outer space. By 1981 almost 2000 military satellites had been launched. Both superpowers are experimenting with methods of destroying one another's missiles and satellites from space. The USA has spent 1.5 billion dollars on laser and beam weapons designed to knock out Soviet ICBMs before they could reach their target. In a test in January 1984, America successfully destroyed a missile in flight, from space. The American programme, nicknamed President Reagan's 'Star Wars' policy, is likely to make future USA–USSR arms talks even more complicated and difficult.

China has not entered into this new phase of the arms race. It is making efforts to modernise its existing forces and to equip its vast army of 4½ million with effective weapons. China's nuclear force consists of some 200 missiles. They seem to exist largely as a deterrent to

E Women peace protesters outside the American missile base at Greenham Common, in Berkshire, England

Russia's interest in China's northern border.

In comparison to China's nuclear force, America and Russia have massive nuclear stockpiles. According to evidence from the United Nations:

❛There are more than 40 000 nuclear warheads in the world today. The total strength is about 1 million Hiroshima bombs . . . every large bomb has a destructive power greater than all explosives ever used since the discovery of gunpowder.❜ (G)

??????????????

1 **a** What would the figures in **A** suggest to military leaders in America?
  b Does **A** confirm NATO's view of Russia (**B**)?

2 **a** Why is outer space becoming increasingly important in the arms race?
  b Explain how new weapons can upset the balance of terror.

3 **a** Why are the women in **E** protesting about the American weapons?
  b Will Cruise weapons make Britain a safer, or a more dangerous, place to live? Discuss.

4 Are the two superpowers involved in another arms race? If so, which country do you think is most responsible for starting it? Give reasons for your answer.

34 Into the Eighties

What is the state of relations between America and Russia in the 1980s?

Photographs **A** to **C** are evidence about events involving East and West since 1980. Study each photograph and caption carefully. If you can remember any of the events shown, try to think back to your feelings at that time.

A On 31 August/1 September 1983 a South Korean Jumbo jet was shot down by Russian fighters. 269 people were killed. President Reagan said 'What can we think of a regime (Government) that commits a terrorist act to sacrifice the lives of innocent human beings.'

B In October 1983 the USA sent a force of Marines to invade the tiny Carribean island of Grenada. The Americans said they had acted to protect Americans living on Grenada, and to remove a left-wing Government hostile to America. Russia described the act as 'international terrorism'. In a speech on American television, President Reagan said 'We got there just in time. Grenada was a Soviet–Cuban colony being readied as a major military base to export terror and undermine democracy.'

C In March 1985 talks between the USA and USSR about the control of nuclear weapons began again in Geneva, Switzerland. The re-election of President Reagan in 1984, and the selection of Mikhail Gorbachev in 1985 as Russia's new leader, raised hopes of better relations between America and Russia.

With a topic like the Great Power Conflict, some of the events you have studied are very recent. In fact, it is often difficult to say where 'History' stops and where 'News' or 'Current Affairs' begins. By the time you read this, new events concerning America, Russia and China will already have happened. Try to find out about them, and about what is happening at the moment, so that you can keep your knowledge of the Great Powers up-to-date.

??????????????

1 a Discuss, in groups, if the events shown in **A** and **B** could be called a new phase of the Cold War.
b Does event **C** suggest any changes in America–Russia relations?

2 Think back to any recent world events involving the Great Powers.
a Discuss what happened and which countries were involved.
b Did the event improve or worsen the Great Power relations?

3 What sources of evidence could you use to write about a very recent (last 12 months) event involving Great Power conflict?

4 What can you do to stay up-to-date with changes in Great Power Conflict?